ALY RICHARDS &
SCOTT McLEAN

INTELLIGENT CUSTOMER ENGAGEMENT

The future of content marketing

The **Intelligent**
Marketing Institute

Published in Great Britain 2014 by
The Intelligent Marketing Institute
www.timihub.com

A CIP catalogue record for this book is available
from the British Library.

Paperback ISBN 978-0-9930211-0-7
Hardback ISBN   978-0-9930211-1-4

Also available as an eBook:
eBook mobi ISBN 978-0-9930211-2-1
eBook epub ISBN 978-0-9930211-3-8

Images by the following contributors within this book have been
sourced through istockphoto.co.uk royalty free photo-library:
© AleksandarNakic | © GlobalStock | © Robert Churchill | © skynesher
© SerrNovik | © fcafotodigital | © londoneye | © Renphoto | © spaxiax
© Lisa-Blue | © jaroon

Designed at Chandler Book Design.

Printed in Great Britain by
Print-On-Demand Worldwide

CONTENTS

How to Use This Book

This book is intended as a manual and reference, you may therefore not read it end-to-end but jump about as required. There may also be chapters on subjects that you are well versed in and feel that you do not need to read, we would suggest you still take a skim through these as we probably provide a challenge to what you think you know or discuss the next evolution of the subject. This book is for a marketing educated reader and is about taking capabilities and technologies on to the next level.

We will be providing case studies, templates and updates online via our website. You can find out more at **www.timihub.com**

Foreword

I cannot think of any individuals who are having a greater beneficial impact on marketing practice than Aly and Scott. I first met Aly when she presented in Cranfield on the inspirational Vision project which she drove at O2. The marketing faculty felt that day that we'd just been shown a glimpse of the future of marketing, and everything I've seen since then confirms that initial excitement. Ten interviews in O2 by a then Cranfield colleague (who is now marketing director at Cisco Services Europe) confirmed the extraordinary reality behind the story. Since then, numerous senior blue-chip marketers have testified to me as to how much they've learned from Aly as she's applied her Intelligent Customer Engagement principles to other client projects. More recently I've also got to know Scott, who shares Aly's passion for a world in which we engage with customers in relevant, content-rich conversations, rather than bombarding them with irrelevant messages

that only train them that we are not worth listening to. They have presented again in Cranfield recently on their inspirational work with a range of blue-chips to make this future happen today. Scott and Aly understand through hard experience how to create business value from customer interactions that are individualised, honest and meaningful, and that put the customer's interests first. Crucially they also have a proven ability to make it happen, not just through technology and processes but also through structure, culture and organisational change. For all of us who don't just believe in the possibility of a genuine, mutually satisfying engagement with our customers but are determined to bring this about, this book is simply essential reading.

Hugh Wilson,
Professor of Strategic Marketing, Cranfield School of Management

SECTION

1

Introduction

The purpose of any commercial organisation is to create a customer, not a product or service. By creating a customer, any organisation is also creating an audience. Maintaining the interest of that audience has now become a recognised business priority as it is only through that interest that the company can hope to maintain the loyalty of that customer. The challenge, as businesses have quickly come to realise, is that creating that audience interest will not simply come from being an interesting company that is doing what is believed to be interesting things with its interesting products or services. That is the old language where audiences were people to be sold **to**. Today an audience is someone to be engaged **with**.

For virtually every commercial organisation in existence today, making this shift to audience engagement is a huge step change. This is because audience engagement does not just mean having a call centre or other aspects of customer service. Instead, engagement is about conversing with the audience in a way that each side finds mutually interesting. The implication is twofold: firstly, brands cannot just keep talking about themselves and secondly, they have got to find compelling content with which to engage the audience.

We call this the 'content-led approach' and this is a phrase we will continually refer to throughout this book.

That is why it is increasingly commonplace for brands to start trying to behave as publishers. Understanding this and implementing it within an organisation is what this book is about. There are many business books that will help you in the basics of marketing, but as it is so fast-moving in terms of the technologies available, these texts are quickly out-dated. Consequently, our aim is to create this book as a dynamic tool that will be updated as the world changes, but which is grounded in some basic principles. You will therefore find more resources online, as well as revisions.

And while this book is about content marketing it is not preoccupied with the creation and delivery of content. Companies have been creating and delivering content not just for years, but for centuries. As a marketer you do not need to be told how to create and deliver content as long as you are perceptive enough to keep up with today's fast changing media world – and by media we mean that in the broadest sense, encapsulating social media and any channel that can be used to reach your target audience.

Instead this book focuses on the strategy that must underpin a content marketing approach. Think of this as two layers. The inner layer is the creation and delivery of the content and defines how you align your existing marketing campaigns and communications programmes within a mature content marketing framework that is designed to deliver very specific business objectives.

The outer layer is how you structurally support this within the organisation so that every customer-facing function within the business is aligned. After all, the lines between sales,

marketing and IT are getting very blurred. This can be highly confusing not only when navigating your own role but also the role of marketing and publishing. Whilst the lines are getting blurred, these departments are often in silos and are not aligned with one another because, more than anything else, they do not really understand each other. Rather than working together for one organisation, these areas often end up as combative. The result is sub-optimal marketing and sub-optimal performance of your company. This book will explain each part of the puzzle in enough detail to break down these barriers so that the business can become centred around your audience, in other words your customers.

Given that taking a content-led approach within an organisation is new to many people, there are sections within this book that take this into consideration as well as more advanced ideas that will help you develop organisational maturity around customer engagement. Some of the solutions that we suggest are technical and require software. It is simply the nature of the world that marketing is now predominately digital. Given that and the rise of the social network, there is no way around the use of technology in your marketing efforts. What we will endeavour to do is provide you with what you need to do and not specify which product you should pick for the job. However, as a guiding principle we suggest that you consider your requirements first (rather than being sold to by a vendor), then see if there are cloud based options for these requirements. The cloud is an excellent way of keeping all your costs down and therefore improving your ROI on marketing investments.

We have also supported this book with tools, methods and templates that we have made available to help you transform your marketing. However, this is meant as a practical reference manual and we will be continually adding to every aspect of this book over time.

Marketing Redefined

First though, a definition of marketing: the art and science of attracting and engaging customers with your brand that will lead to sales of your products and services. This definition is not necessarily the standard definition you may find in the textbooks but as we have seen the lines blur; this definition helps to clarify who is doing what. What we have found all too often is that marketing is performing sales and IT functions or in many cases is treated as a subordinate service to those departments. We intend to call that out and while it may be that you wish to leave things where they are after considering our points, at least you can now be informed about that decision and make sure that it is the most optimal way for your business to be run.

This blurring occurs because people are usually, and with good intent, just trying to get something done or delivered. For a couple of examples, firstly look at the implementation of Decision Engines in contact centres. If you are not familiar with Decision Engines, they are advanced systems for contact centres that use insight about the customer to provide the advisor with intelligent decisions about what to say to the customer within the call. This means that rather than simply thinking about what to sell to that customer, the advisor can put the needs of the customer first and in so doing make the right decision at the right time for the right customer. Putting any technical complexities to one side, most people would agree that organisations should strive to do this, especially when they learn that conversion rates are considerably higher over the lifecycle of a customer when such an approach is taken. But the question is, who should be responsible for initiating such a project? Marketing? Sales? IT?

Interestingly, these initiatives have mostly been run as marketing or CRM projects. Yet firstly, if you look at the processes being managed, these are actually sales processes to existing customers. So, if we return to our definition, marketing is about getting the customer to this point, not closing the deal. Secondly, often these projects involve deployments of applications and data, such as warehouses and campaign management tools within marketing, that have been deployed without the involvement of IT or because marketing has chosen to turn to external agencies just because it is quicker and easier than using the internal IT department. However, eventually this silo approach will lead to sub-optimal performance for the organisation and sub-optimal engagement levels with customers. All this crossing the lines is then made worse if we consider engagement as a long-term relationship effort and not just to the point of sale. Marketing should therefore continue after the sale in order to continue the engagement.

Another example comes from the world of B2B marketing. All too often B2B marketers operate in an entirely divorced world from their sales colleagues who, in turn, view marketing as little more than a service function. At its most strategic, marketing and communications may be seen as a lead enabler but at the opposite end of the scale, marketing is often relegated to the role of collateral creation and 'fluffy stuff'. All of this assumes that there is no prior engagement between the brand and the prospective customer before he or she enters the sales funnel. Where that might have been true once, it is most certainly not true today. Every customer started as someone who had a view about your company, even if that view was wrong or one of total ignorance.

Every external activity undertaken by marketing impacts that view until they become a qualified lead and enter the funnel. No one ever enters the funnel without a prior journey having taken place and therefore marketing and sales should never be divorced, rather they should be intimately joined at the hip.

However, let us also consider that a customer is not a customer, they are a person. Sounds obvious enough, but when you get down in the weeds of marketing or sales then the term 'customer' becomes some abstract creature that is a collection of data attributes that we have to 'treat'. We then go to war and start 'targeting' them in 'campaigns'; all pretty aggressive when you think about it. The human element gets lost in the processes of marketing and sales. Our premise is that before the customer is a customer, and even when they are a customer, they are your audience.

So this takes us back to the point that as an audience they need to be engaged 'with'. This is in contrast to the typical approach today where audiences are targets that brands broadcast 'at' or sell 'to'. This goes with the historic obsession with message delivery to the right target segment. Even the recent shift to storytelling within some advertising campaigns is only being done to create an emotional reaction for the purpose of campaign conversion, not as a means of generating genuine sustained brand engagement. The problem is that to shift from the broadcast mentality to an engagement approach you need to evolve the nature of marketing away from sequential, disconnected, standalone campaigns. The key to achieving that is content.

The Content Coronation

The phrase 'content is king' has been doing the rounds in marketing communications circles for quite some time and many people have become a bit tired of hearing about it. However, the truth is that content is not yet king but remains the heir apparent as traditional approaches have clung to the throne. But, casting analogies firmly to one side, is it right to even talk about content marketing as being something new?

The reality is that we have all been doing content marketing for years, just without necessarily recognising it as such. At the end of the day, any piece of content that you as a marketer have been putting out by e-mail, through advertising, in a brochure, definitely through PR and, dare we say it, through DM through the post, has in essence been a form of content marketing. Furthermore, for those who see content marketing as an approach that suddenly turns a brand into a publisher, then you only need to look at the numerous magazines that companies have been producing for many, many years – our favourite being Furrow from John Deere for no reason other than the fact that the authors of this book both live in the countryside!

But the way content marketing can be done today **has** changed. It is for that reason that the examples given above are not what is meant by content marketing today.

The digital revolution has had a profound impact on the way in which a brand can engage with its audience. It means there is direct action and interaction, often in real-time. This means that the content that a brand produces within a marketing campaign need not be standalone but can link to other content and not necessarily content that you have had to create yourselves – welcome to the world of user-generated content.

It is this seismic shift that allows companies to become customer-centric, not simply brand or product-centric. In other words, rather than simply telling your customer base what you would like them to hear, you can now provide them with mutually interesting content that they would welcome. And you will know that they do, indeed, welcome it because you will be able to see and hear their reaction in real-time. We have gone from the world of brand monologue to brand dialogue (conversation).

So content marketing is about putting your customer, not yourselves, at the heart of your marketing communications strategy and integrating this editorialised approach across all your marketing communications. This means that you need to have a content strategy that will help you create compelling stories that your customers will be interested in.

A simplistic example would be that if you are a bank selling mortgages then your current approach to content will revolve around how clear and compelling the sales message is around your existing products. However, if you were to take a customer-centric content marketing approach, you would seek to understand what you and your target audience have in common that your target audience might like to read about or watch; one obvious example might be property (instead of mortgages). So rather than broadcasting at your target audience about how wonderful your latest mortgage products are, what you could be talking about is planning law, how to choose a good builder, what sort of insulation is best for a 1970s property and so on and so forth. This is because a content marketing strategy that provides genuinely useful content for that property buyer and, for the long-term, property owner is likely to lead to a fruitful engagement and relationship which will see brand loyalty and customer insight increase, and opportunities to sell, retain, and cross-sell dramatically increase.

It may or may not be obvious for you to see how that could apply to your brand and your audience. However, whether you are a B2C or B2B company, the opportunity to create and tell a compelling and engaging story always exists.

But, why take a content-led approach? The answer to that question really depends on your brand and your objectives. In the example just given it will almost certainly be because conversion rates will be better – more consumers will be fed into the sales funnel, you will lose fewer customers out of your funnel, more sales will be made, customers' loyalty will increase and the value per customer will increase accordingly. For other brands it might be because customer insight is poor and a content-led approach is the most compelling way to overcome that challenge. Or it could be because brand awareness is the number one priority and content marketing is a more effective way of creating an engaging above the line or below the line campaign.

And to that last point, adopting a content-led approach to your customer engagement neither excludes nor prioritises any particular form of marketing communications activity. Perhaps the only major impact it will have is to challenge the campaign-led approach to marketing as being somewhat redundant in a world of sustained engagement. To that end, the symptom that most organisations face of having a 'leaky bucket' when it comes to the sales funnel, will be better understood and mitigated.

What it will lead to is a greater understanding of the customer, greater engagement and because of that a demonstrable ROI.

Fighting the Silo

If taking a content-led approach will be evolutionary for the marketing function, it will be revolutionary for the business. Or at least it will be if all the required steps towards content marketing strategy maturity are taken.

The reality of any commercial organisation is that no single department or function within the business is the custodian of customer engagement. Perhaps this should not be the case and organisations should be entirely restructured to put the customer first and every other department and function designed from that point outwards? However, that is nothing but idle speculation. The realpolitik of the situation is that moving to a content-led approach for customer engagement will not work if purely delivered within and through the marketing function. Instead, every customer engagement function must be considered.

Of course, breaking down the silos and behaving in an integrated fashion has been debated, tried, tested and proven largely unsuccessful time and time again. This is because every function still has its own objectives and business requirements that it must fulfil and no single process is going to knit these conflicting interests together. The answer, therefore, is not to try to integrate them at all.

Instead, the answer is to align them around the customer engagement itself, in other words by using an 'audience engagement strategy' built around content as the glue that binds these diverse functions together. To give just one example, today no organisation has ever successfully integrated their inbound and outbound customer engagement functions. Many have, of course, tried but the fundamental problem they have always encountered is that the data and processes that govern the way you try to capture a customer through an outbound marketing campaign is entirely different to that of an inbound customer engagement into a contact centre or digital channel. There are simply very few points of direct data and process convergence around which an integration can take place and the return on investment by making the monumental effort of making it happen just does not stack up.

However, you **can** integrate inbound and outbound by using an audience engagement strategy built around content as the common point of integration. The reason being that it is the content that both the organisation and the audience have in common and the only differences for outbound and inbound, to put them in their correct sequence, will be where the audience is on their individual journeys.

The startling revelation for marketers will be that the result of taking a content-led engagement approach is to elevate marketing up within the organisation. The reason is simple: the organisation must realign itself around the customer, and marketing is the custodian of the content strategy that governs the engagement journey between the brand and the audience at all times – in other words marketing designs, delivers and reports on the audience engagement strategy.

Of course, achieving this paradigm shift will not be easy and it will not happen overnight. It will also require new skills and capabilities to be invested in. However, the most important point to recognise for any marketer taking this path is that to achieve a successful, mature, content-led approach to audience engagement, you are going to have to take your internal stakeholders on a journey themselves. It really is a case of 'physician, heal thyself'. In other words,

before starting on a seismic change to the way the organisation engages customers, start by taking your own internal audience on a journey first. In reality this will happen concurrently, but the point is that it does have to happen.

Of All the Five Ws, the One That Matters Most: Why?

You have now reached the point where you will be deciding whether or not to commit to reading this book in full. Is it right for you? In other words is it relevant and can you practically make use of it? This is, after all, a business book and its value will be largely derived from its usefulness within your working life. So let's answer the only genuinely important question: why take a content-led approach to audience engagement?

The answer lies in a perfect storm of factors that have already led trailblazers such as Red Bull, Coca-Cola and British Gas to adopt this approach.

The first point to make is, naturally enough, regarding the audience. Or, more importantly, the changing relationship between your audience and your organisation. Today, how customers perceive their relationship with a company largely determines their brand loyalty and the potential profitability of the relationship. Consequently, companies need to create personalised, unique and engaging experiences, products, services and advice for each customer if they are to successfully maintain and grow the relationship.

The traditional method used to get the audience's attention and increase willingness to buy has been to bombard them with campaigns, messages and marketing materials through the mail, television, billboards, online, by telephone, etc. This method is broad-spectrum, designed to put corporate-driven messages in front of as many customers as possible. And, to a large extent, these messages continue to follow the four principles of marketing that have been around since the 1960s – product, place, price and promotion. While there is a need to establish a product and brand presence, these methods are proving steadily less successful as companies find much of the material is ignored. What we aim to show with this book is how you can evolve from this point of maturity to owning a truly engaged audience.

More recently, sales and marketing have improved campaigns by targeting specific groups with the aim of lowering the volume and increasing the response rate. However, success is typically measured by volume and not necessarily by the results from all that communication. Sales do occur but, barraged with communications through

many channels, people have learned to ignore most outbound marketing efforts. Response rates to these campaigns illustrate the problem: a response rate of 5% for direct mail is considered an outstanding result, but often rates are much lower even for a 'targeted' campaign.

The problem lies in the fact that this approach to interacting with audiences does not take into account the individual's point of view. Simply put, companies need to become more 'customer-centric' by delivering compelling experiences that do not just fulfil, but exceed expectations. To do so, companies must rethink the audience engagement cycle so that they view each customer as an asset and every interaction an as opportunity to increase the value of that asset. Conversely, every interaction is also an opportunity to decrease the asset value if the message and approach is wrong. Thinking back to the highly regarded 5% response rate for a typical marketing campaign, this means that 95% did not respond. When we consider that audience as assets, then the non-response rate of 95% represents a significant reduction in their asset value. Most companies seem not to care about this potential self-inflicted brand damage.

Creating a unique and lasting audience experience is the critical factor for building brand loyalty, customer retention and profitability. While customers remain mostly satisfied with fast, efficient service and effective protection of data and assets, you can only enhance the value and longevity of the customer relationship by delivering a set of experiences that focus on the needs of individuals.

This is why implementing a comprehensive strategy for managing audience engagement via a content-led approach is now crucial. At every phase of the audience journey – from prospecting and acquisition to service and retention – companies need to deliver intentional content that puts the audience's interests at the heart of each interaction and creates engagement.

The second point is with regards to your brand reputation and who, in reality, controls it. The answer is: **not** you. Actually that answer is only correct if you are reading this with your corporate marketer hat on. If you are reading this as an ordinary consumer in relation to the multitude of brands you have a view about on a daily basis, or indeed as B2B purchaser, then the answer is actually: **you** do.

The fact is that it is not what a company does or does not do that impacts the brand reputation but the view of the consumer in relation to that action; and brand reputation really, really matters when it comes to purchasing decisions. If your product is deemed to be poor then its bad reputation, more than anything else, will lead to poor sales. This applies equally at a corporate brand level. Did Nokia's mobile phone division fail simply because it failed to keep up with smartphone product development? On the one hand yes it did, but the reputation it gained as the mobile phone manufacturer that had failed to keep up with smartphone development was equally as important. It would have taken a game-changing product that would have got people talking to catch up with Apple and Samsung. Again, it would not just have been the hypothetical product but the reputation that product would have had that could have saved Nokia. Of course that is history now as it did not produce that game-changing product and it has now been swallowed up by Microsoft for a fraction of what its market value would once have been.

And this brings us on to the third point: the way people engage has changed. As with so many things in life, this is all down to digital. Any brand can be a publisher today because the barriers to entry are relatively low. No longer does content marketing involve producing a monthly magazine with all the associate production, printing and distribution costs. Create a video, stick it on YouTube for free. Create a Facebook or Twitter account and build an audience. Create a microsite and host a forum. All of these activities can be done for a fraction of the cost; however, they will only succeed if the content strategy that underpins them is both audience-centric and connected to specific business goals. That is why, as we will see within the book, so many content strategies are failing to deliver today.

That failure is also linked, as mentioned earlier, to the fact that any brand experience created through digital channels must be followed through across the entire audience engagement. It is no use creating an image and expectation in digital channels and then failing to replicate that experience across all customer touch-points. As far as the audience is concerned, you are one brand regardless of how they choose to engage with you.

However, most importantly digital has changed the way people both talk about brands and interact with brands. As we will discuss in more depth within this book, it has never been so easy for an individual to publicise their own views about a brand. Equally importantly, it has never been easier for a brand to engage with its audience. Digital, not simply social media, has been the enabler of this. It remains the ultimate game-changer.

The Way Forward

The following chapters will step through the model describing how to realign your business around engaging your audience using content within an audience engagement strategy. Our name for this new paradigm for businesses is Intelligent Customer Engagement (ICE).

ICE is not CRM (Customer Relationship Management) or the more mature CEM (Customer Experience Management). Where CRM is enterprise-focused and designed to manage customers for maximum efficiency, ICE is a strategy that focuses the operations and processes of a business around the intelligent engagement of individuals.

Nor is ICE a straightforward content strategy run as a part of an outbound marketing campaign. And it certainly is not confined only to social media and the digital channels, although those channels are important. Instead it is about audience-centricity, understanding the entire journey a target audience will take with your organisation. It is vital to understand that the use of content as the engagement mechanism with audiences is the foundation of this paradigm shift but at the same time is also nothing more than the tool that enables the structural change from your organisation being product and/or service-centric to being truly customer-centric.

As such, you will see within this book how ICE achieves the following:

- **ICE and customer perception:**

  You know that customers are looking for 'feel good' experiences in their relationships with you. The role of ICE is to develop processes that engender a positive perception each time a customer touches the company. By delivering engaging experiences across the customer lifecycle, the company engenders a collection of positive perceptions that build brand loyalty, provide clear differentiation and increase the value of the company to the customer.

- **ICE and customer processes:**

  Customer-facing processes used to be about efficiency and volume – reduce call time, push out as many direct mail pieces as possible. In the ICE model, process focuses on the experiences each customer has with the company throughout the customer lifecycle from pre-purchase information consumption, through purchase, to post-purchase service via multiple channels. Process, then, becomes the vehicle by which companies create the feel-good experiences. ICE requires that processes are designed to take into account their effects on customers and employees. Each process must be tailored to the individual customer to ensure a positive experience. At the same time, each process must also be designed so that the employee can engage with the customer in ways that are consistently positive, reinforcing and successful. It is about being able to have conversations with individuals and not just shouting louder at a mass you call customers.

- **ICE and brand identification:**

  Traditionally, brand is thought of as that which differentiates a business, and this differentiation is conveyed through the presentation of the company to the consumer world via advertising, promotions, package design and so forth. But in the new ICE world, brand has become much more than just the business's physical face. Today, the perception each customer forms of the company and its products based on his or her aggregate engaging experiences is crucial to building brand. It also adds fuel to the need for companies to take greater care of their external reputation.

The challenge when implementing an ICE strategy is to create experiences that amplify the customer's estimation of brand through intentional and consistent delivery of brand-specific experiences across all touch points. The question 'Are we on-brand?' must not only be asked about each ad or promotion, but each interaction. The process must be tailored to both the individual and the brand so that the customer experiences the brand throughout the interaction. When branding is built into the customer experience, organisations can achieve the ultimate goal – customers who consistently perceive value in the company's brand – leading to the greater loyalty and lifetime value that generates long-term profitability from their audience.

ICE and Business Outcome

Ultimately ICE is about achieving improvements across a number of key metrics, such as conversion rates, reputation, sales uplift and loyalty. However, these outcomes will be determined by your business priorities. At the same time, ICE should be implemented in an evolutionary way, not as a revolution. Businesses are too complex and the relationships with prospects and customers too multifaceted to support overnight change. Not that ICE needs such an approach.

As you will see within this book, ICE has a logical implementation approach that will allow any organisation of any size, be it B2C or B2B, to mature towards Intelligent Customer Engagement within Business As Usual.

SECTION

2

What is a Content Marketing Strategy?

As you will have noted from the introductory chapter, the key tool within the Intelligent Customer Engagement approach is the use of content. As you will also be fully aware, content marketing has already become a fairly commonplace term within the world of marketing and communications. If the way agencies and consultancies position themselves can be viewed as a barometer of trends, then you could easily argue that content marketing itself has already become ubiquitous. This is no surprise given, as we have already argued, that content marketing has been around since the earliest days of marketing in one guise or another, as well as the fact that digital has provided the catalyst for its elevation to the top of the marketing tree. The problem is that everyone is using the term 'content marketing' in different ways.

Having a multitude of interpretations is, of course, pretty normal for 'big new things'. Everyone wants to twist a concept to fit their particular set of skills and capabilities. Quite right too, as how can anyone truly claim ownership of an idea? However, it does leave the poor marketer having to navigate this sea of differing ideas. You will note that we do not say 'conflicting ideas' and that is because 99% of the time, the way in which the term 'content marketing' is being interpreted is actually nothing more than one aspect of the whole.

However, we do recognise that to understand what you are looking for, you need to understand what is available and so in an effort to help codify the world of content marketing we use three core terms and definitions.

Content Marketing

This is the use of content within any marketing activity, campaign or programme. It is not limited to any specific channel, media or approach. As such, anything from a printed magazine, to an e-shot, TV advert, B2B thought leadership campaign or owned media website falls within the catchment of content marketing. For the avoidance of doubt, social media also falls within this bracket. Content marketing is, if you like, the creation and delivery of content within any marketing or communications activity. This is why, as many commentators point out, content marketing is really as old as the hills.

You will therefore encounter a wide range of tools that claim to help deliver content marketing even though they do quite different things. The fact is that they are all relevant and, depending on your needs, can support you in a variety of different ways. For example, an online content curation tool sits comfortably alongside a campaign automation tool.

Content Strategy

However, content marketing should not be confused with a content strategy. Nor is the difference between the two as simple as saying that any marketing and communications activity naturally requires an overarching strategy. Instead, a content strategy is the overarching plan for delivering a content marketing programme and although that may appear relatively straightforward, what has emerged is a myriad of interpretations as to what that involves.

At the one extreme are those who simply see it as the planning of what content should be created and delivered and ideally (which unfortunately means not always) which channels it should be delivered through. At the more mature end of the spectrum, where our thinking lies, are those that see a content strategy as being about making the planning, creation, delivery and measurement of content the red thread that runs through all your marketing activities. In other words, that the content strategy is not simply limited to one isolated set of activities, such as your social media programme. Instead it is a single strategy that is executed across everything you do.

Most importantly, the planning and measurement elements of the content strategy allow you to take carefully identified audiences on pre-defined journeys that will meet your business goals – e.g. reputation turnaround; sales uplift; etc. – and then be able to measure your success in achieving this through the content that is consumed.

Audience Engagement Strategy

Yet as you will have seen from the opening section of this book, we believe that the weakness of current thinking around content marketing is that limiting it to the marketing function completely misses the point about customer engagement. As we have already argued, the customer engages with the brand, not an aspect of the brand in a single channel. As such, if a mature content strategy is going to take the audience on a complete journey, then the content must be seeded across all customer touch-points and this stretches beyond the marketing function.

That is why we refer to an audience engagement strategy, in other words the wider content-led approach that will see every customer engagement touch-point integrated around the content strategy. It also deliberately puts content in its place – content is just a tool! It is not, despite what you might read or hear elsewhere, anything other than that. The obsession with creating and delivering great content is a major barrier to success and so you will see that we quite deliberately stress the importance of the audience, for which content is the tool through which you can engage them.

Therefore it does not matter whether you as the audience have called in through the contact centre, responded to a piece of e-mail

marketing, engaged through social media, or simply watched an ad on television, your single journey with the brand will be governed by a single audience engagement strategy.

This is more than simple semantics, this is an entire approach that will transform the organisation into one that is truly customer-centric in deed and not just word. Achieving this transformation is relatively complex and that is why we have developed our Intelligent Customer Engagement (ICE) methodology that we will be explaining within this book.

It is worth pointing out that our intention in providing clarity around these definitions is not because we expect the industry to align around those terms. However, we do hope that it helps you charter the content marketing seas when it comes to interpreting what people are saying and offering. Of course, titles alone will not suffice and that is why the maturity model will help. That chapter is designed to help you understand where you are currently and why you may wish to progress further.

What that, of course, comes down to is the need for a business case. Given the degree of change and investment (in time alone) that will be required to transition towards an audience engagement strategy approach, starting with the business case makes sense. However, for the time being you will encounter one major challenge when doing this: it's all fairly new. And with the word 'new' comes the fact that there are not many real-world reference points to base any ROI projections upon. Depending on your appetite for risk, this may prove an insurmountable obstacle for many people.

However, do remember that adopting a content-led approach in general is an evolution not a revolution. You will be doing some aspects of content marketing within your marketing and communications function already. You may also have a content strategy. All of this can be improved incrementally. That is common-sense structural maturity with limited requirement for investment, just a sound rationale around the objectives you are seeking to meet. Section three will show you how to do this, however; first you need to understand what changes will be involved internally.

In this chapter

- Immediate Challenges

All Change

For modern companies, change has become business as usual. Be it due to fluctuating economic conditions, market disruption or the emergence of new technologies, businesses are perpetually having to react to external forces that force a shift from the status quo, let alone the internal innovations and investments that equally drive change. However despite this, dealing with change and forecasting how challenging initiatives will necessitate widespread change across the organisation will be an intimidating prospect. Therefore in the spirit of 'know your enemy', we are going to delve into a number of typical challenges you will face when contemplating a shift towards greater audience engagement maturity.

The reasons we are doing so at this stage is because we believe it is best to put these challenges firmly on the table now before going into the detail of what can be done and how compelling the results can be. After all, human nature errs towards fear, uncertainty and doubt (often called the FUD factor) first before rationalising the facts and considering a logical way forward. It is for this reason that within the art of storytelling, which is a key component of a mature content marketing strategy as you will see later, the order of engaging an audience is to first identify with their lives today (the 'Ordinary World'), then to excite them with something new (the 'Call to Adventure') before acknowledging that their next reaction will be to find reasons to not try something new (the 'Refusal of the Call'). So in the spirit of eating our own dog food, let's deal with **your** own potential 'Refusal of the Call'.

We Already Do Content Marketing and Have a Content Strategy

Having looked at the definitions outlined in the previous chapter, you may feel that the content marketing and associated content strategy that you already have in place is satisfactory. Obviously only you can determine this and to aid you in making that judgement we would encourage you to self-assess your content marketing maturity by reading the next chapter.

However, in short there are four key points that you will need to determine. First of all, does your content strategy straddle all relevant channels? Typically, and quite rightly, a content strategy begins (and ends) in a single channel and often this is within digital. However, your audience does not think, feel and act in one channel when it comes to you and your brand so is it appropriate for your content strategy to be constrained in this fashion?

This, of course, takes us on to the second point which we made quite clearly in the previous chapter and which forms the basis of section four of this book; namely, the fact that the content strategy needs to be enterprise-wide across all customer engagement touch-points. However, this is a new concept that is fraught with its own challenges so we will cover this off in more detail further on within this chapter.

The third point to make is regards the purpose of your existing content strategy. All too often the content strategy exists to simply serve a channel such as digital or, to make the point more critically, to have a Twitter account because the company feels it should have one. The problem, as we all know, is that social media has an insatiable hunger for content and feeding that content beast can quickly become a major headache. The natural response is to create a content strategy that is built around an editorial calendar that allows you to tame the beast. Suddenly you have structure to the way the content is being produced and a regular pattern of content creation and platform management ensues.

This is all quite appropriate and the right thing to do...up to a point; and that point is quite simply to ask yourself what is the purpose of the resulting content strategy? If the strategy is to simply provide workable structure for a digital channel that you have decided to communicate through, then that is content problem-solving, not content strategy. To be strategic it must have a purpose and that should be centred around influencing the target audience to think, feel or do something different. It is for this reason that the content strategy approach that we recommend (i.e. what we call the audience engagement strategy) uses the art of storytelling to take any target audience on a pre-determined journey that they find mutually advantageous.

The art of storytelling is an example of the final point worth making around the question of whether your existing content strategy requires change. Content marketing in its current form is relatively new but maturing rapidly. As such, fresh approaches, developments, hints, tips and tricks are emerging constantly which can help improve what you may already have in place. Evolution not revolution is our mantra when it comes to content marketing and we strongly encourage you to take a similar approach.

We Do Not Have the Internal Resource to Produce More Content

This is an incredibly valid point and one we will return to in section three on content strategy alignment. If, as stated above, you have already begun content marketing in the form of running a social media account, then you will have already faced the conundrum of content creation resourcing. To deal with social media channels alone, many companies outsource the content creation to their marketing and PR agencies, make a hire or, where possible, add it to an existing member of staff's role requirement. Sadly this often means that content creation is being

handled by a fairly junior member of staff and by default lacks strategy. And yet this only solves the problem of handling content creation within a single channel.

The fact is that managing a content marketing programme and producing the required content will require resource investment. That may be in the form of technology to curate the content alongside what you already create. It may also be in the form of external agencies that specialise in content creation. However, as we will discuss later on, you may also find yourself having to develop a dedicated editorial team to manage the production, creation and execution process. To justify this, of course, you will need a business case.

We Have a Number of Content Strategy Initiatives Emerging Within the Company

This is an increasingly common occurrence and is symptomatic of the current shift to customer-centric engagement (as opposed to product/service-centric engagement). It is therefore only natural that any function within the business that deals with any form of audience engagement could start to introduce a content framework to their work.

The key point here is that this is not necessarily a negative development. By evolving your audience engagement strategy over time, you will be aligning existing processes and structures around any existing content strategies. This allows different parts of the audience engagement process to embark on their own paths and initiatives without necessarily creating conflict. Of course there is a massive caveat within that sentence: the word 'necessarily'.

At the end of the day, if we accept that the audience only sees one brand regardless of how you are internally structured, then any form of content engagement must not clash with another form of content engagement in a different channel. This is common-sense and mirrors the approach businesses have always taken to product/service messaging since time immemorial – i.e. that there will only ever be one set of messaging used consistently across the organisation. In the same way, any forms of content engagement within the business must be aligned, ideally with a single owner of the crucial 'points of mutuality' and 'content pillars' – see section three for more details. From our perspective, it should be the marketing department that has this ownership because it is the marketing function that has greater points of connection with the audience, from the earliest stages of prospect attraction and brand awareness raising, through to loyalty and retention.

We Do Not Have the Authority To Align the Other Functions

It is extremely unlikely that a decision to align the other functions will be made and therefore mandated by the CEO or board. However, what we are seeing within organisations and their leadership is a seismic shift towards customer-centricity; although worth stressing that from an audience engagement strategy perspective, this should actually be **audience**-centricity in order to take into account the fact that the target audience's journey starts before they make any form of purchase and are not yet a 'customer'. Yet the fact remains that while any mandate towards putting the customer first may come from the top, the means to making this happen will come from within functional layers below.

The challenge here could be quite daunting for the unambitious. First of all you are going to have to initiate change within the marketing function to align existing activities around the audience engagement strategy. In practice this is about putting in place the correct processes, procedures and structure, with the necessary training to ensure the capabilities are there to allow your team to perform effectively.

If transitioning your own marketing function looks like a potential headache, then the next part of the challenge will seem like a veritable migraine. The fact is that all audience engagement touch-points need to be aligned and integrated through the audience engagement strategy and to do this most marketers will have to persuade, not dictate.

To take just two examples, one each from the B2C and B2B worlds. If your B2C organisation sends out bills then this is a vital audience engagement touch-point that cannot be ignored. However, what goes into those bill envelopes or e-mails does not fall within the marketing function's remit.

From a B2B perspective the challenge is universally the same: how to align sales with marketing. This is an age-old problem but one that becomes even more acute within an audience engagement strategy approach. The audience journey straddles both marketing and sales and it is utterly unviable for the two not to be aligned within a single strategy.

And what if you share a master brand for your division? For example, from an external audience perspective Samsung is just Samsung. Internally this is far from the case and yet even if you align all of the audience engagement functions within your division, what do you do about all the other divisions that share your brand and may have their own content being produced and disseminated? It has to be said that at the time of writing the answer to this challenge is far from clear.

However, what is clear is that the answer to all these challenges almost certainly lies in applying an audience engagement strategy internally as well. This is both a case of practicing what you preach or, as we like to say, eating your own dog food, as well as the fact that content strategies are just as relevant within internal communications as they are for external communications.

This Sounds Like a Significant Investment

It is true that very little change occurs without investment, both of time and money. However, once again we must stress that, predominantly, implementing an audience engagement strategy is about alignment with existing activities rather than replacing or reinventing.

Where investment will be required will be in three areas. First of all manual management of a content strategy would be time-consuming and foolhardy when it extends beyond individual channels. As such, automated audience engagement management systems will be required which can be used across all touch-points.

Tied to this is the second area of investment, which is the technological integration of the existing tools for audience engagement – e.g. outbound marketing, inbound contact centre management systems, inbound digital platforms and most importantly: data.

Finally there is the time to develop the audience engagement strategy, extend it across the enterprise and then maintain it. From a people perspective, this will not be the only investment that could be required – for example, you may need to develop a content production team and audience strategists – however, it will certainly be the most critical.

As ever, the most crucial question you will face is the business case. That is why section five of this book is devoted to business outcomes which we hope will help you to define and develop the business case for your organisation. However, this is not a mature area of marketing for which case studies can be produced containing attractive ROI numbers. Instead, this is an approach which businesses are being attracted to like moths to a flame and unfortunately many are being sucked in without any clear understanding of what is right for their business, regardless of what the long-term business benefits might be. Understanding where your business is on the road to ICE and what level of maturity is right for your business is, therefore, a more important consideration at this stage.

Maturity Model

You would never embark on a journey without both knowing where you are going to and also where you are starting from. Pretty obvious stuff and that is why we have devoted this entire chapter to a maturity model for Intelligent Customer Engagement. We have put it this early in the book because we want you to be able to refer back to it as you progress through sections three and four. As such, and perhaps quite unusally, we actually recommend that you skim read the three sections of this chapter for now. Just absorb the basis of what we are saying and then refer back to it later on when you have fully grasped the essence of this book. What we believe you will find is that your first estimate of where you are in the maturity model spectrum and, more importantly, where you believe your organisation should be may well change having read through the book. When you think about it, this understanding is vital, as how can you create a plan for business change unless you know where you are starting from and where you wish to end up?

So what we have developed for you within this chapter of the book is a maturity model that you can relate your own business to. As a basis for this, we will begin by outlining the principles the maturity model is based around.

The Principles of the Maturity Model

In order to achieve 'best practice' in Intelligent Customer Engagement we have devised ten principles. The principles are business behaviours, practices and capabilities that when put in place properly will significantly improve the organisation's bottom line. All of these principles have been tested and validated as to their effect on company performance.

The principles are arranged into two dimensions that form the model. The purpose of creating the model from these principles is to create a benchmark and a measurement for where you are – your start point. Once you have an accurate view of your current position it is much easier to plan your roadmap to improve so that you can reach your desired destination.

Measurement of maturity against this best practice is determined by five levels, with level five being the highest. Whilst there is a score for each principle and each dimension, you do not have to have a perfect score on everything to reach a level five; indeed, as a business it is not practical to have a perfect score. Instead, it is best to balance implementing certain capabilities against your business model, size and requirements. As we will discuss in business outcomes, the case for any capability implementation is unique to your business. Also, do not assume that you need to achieve a level five in your business at all. It has to be what is appropriate to the levels of engagement that will improve the KPIs for your business.

The model can be used as a benchmark for assessing where you are and identifying where you will get the best bang for your buck by implementing certain capabilities or changing the way that you operate. By taking your organisation through the benchmark you will get:

- a place to start;
- a common language and a shared vision;
- a framework for prioritising actions;
- a way to define what improvement means for your organisation;
- a way to define the case for change.

Maturity Levels

The maturity levels are a layered framework showing a progression from transactional systems that have little or no relationship to customer engagement, to systems that provide complete organisation-wide command and control over all customer interactions and engagement.

The maturity levels, principles and the model have been validated through research. Results from the completed research are shared later.

The Principles – Overview

The following 10 principles are the elements upon which optimal customer engagement can be built.

1. **Individuality.** The use of predictive insight, customer profiling and content consumption insight allows each customer/prospect to be engaged with as an individual.

2. **Audience-centricity.** Audience-centric principles are leveraged in the design of interaction strategies that match actions/messages to audiences, not audiences to actions/messages.

3. **Dynamic interactions.** Continuous (re) assessments of the individual's journey, dynamically guide customer dialogue and match the conversational context (in real-time when appropriate).

4. **Interactive product/service configurability.** Bi-directional negotiation in real-time channels is used to arrive at agreement with a customer/prospect.

5. **Customer selectivity.** Solutions can be individualised based on the long term value of a customer, which is calculated by considering current profitability and predicted future profitability.

6. **Holistic & actionable audience view.** Data is structured around audience attributes rather than around products or processes. Offering a holistic view of the audience that can be leveraged to engage in any channel.

7. **Consistency & unification.** Multiple channels are guided by a centralised audience authority – this is technology process and organisation.

8. **Process orchestration.** Front-office decisions are tied to back-office processes to ensure seamless end-to-end process management.

9. **Relationship management.** Holistic customer/audience strategy plans, transcending silos and channels, are designed to maximise the relationship and bottom line. For example: inbound and outbound channels joined in cross-functional collaboration to design and manage strategic customer marketing/engagement plans.

10. **Command & control.** There is an audience engagement strategy that allows complete planning of the audience journey. There is zero time-to-market for changes to the plan – simulate the business impact, then deploy, monitor, and control changes in real-time; this requires integration to all delivery capabilities.

In this chapter

- Maturity Model Principles

Maturity Model
PART I: Principles

Let's look at those principles in more detail. The ten principles are applied differently to 'customers' and to 'the audience' as this is about inbound versus outbound, as we discussed earlier. Inbound customer engagement is when an existing customer contacts you and starts the interation – this is not restricted to any particular channel. Outbound audience engagement is what you are publishing (that includes advertising, e-mail marketing, web pages, blogs, events and so on), and will be for your prospects, the general public, stakeholders and your customers. As the latter may not be known to you, the data that you have to act on will be different, as will your approach and the content.

> The following descriptions give you more detail on each of the principles.

Individuality

Individuality means that you are not treating your audience as one amorphous mass. That is not as simple as it first seems if you have a large, complex organisation with lots of processes and lots of customers. To be a 'mature' organisation in respect of this principle, your organisation would have the following capabilities:

- Each engagement can be tailored to the individual and it must be perceived as such by the recipient. This is not simply an agent greeting the customer by name or putting the name at the top of an e-mail or letter. It requires that the needs and objectives of the individual, as expressed by them in the current interaction as well as their history and past interactions, govern the flow of the conversation, the actions taken, offers made and content delivered. By leveraging large amounts of known customer data from multiple sources, applying predictive insight, and bringing the resulting decisions accurately into play through logical interpretation at the point of interaction, each customer can be treated as an individual, with all aspects of the experience based on that individual.

- On interactions where the individual is contacting you, data is captured about why they contacted you and this is then used to manage the interaction. Sounds simple enough, but many organisations do not treat the contact as a conversation, merely a transaction. As such, you do not get the best result out of the interaction.

- All current and historical transactions pertaining to each individual customer can be identified. This includes understanding their content consumption and their content engagement journey. This information is fed back in real-time to the audience engagement strategy. The engagement planner will track the individual's journey against one or more personas, and one individual may be on multiple journeys with you. We can tell what journey or journeys the individual is on by what content they consume. The persona will have a goal for both the individual and the company.

- On outbound communications we know what piece of content comes next by referencing the engagement strategy/maps.

- Service levels are set appropriately by the individual customer.

- Predictive insight, content consumption tracking and customer profiling are used to give each customer a unique identity to the organisation.

- In contact centres, calls can be routed to agents based on an individualised assessment of the customer's needs.

- Cross/up-sell offers are made based on an individualised assessment of all available insight about the customer, including past and predicted behaviours.

- Investment in individual customers is matched to the probable value that the customer will bring to the organisation.

Audience-Centricity

Being audience-centric as an organisation sounds obvious enough. However, as your business grows you often develop silos between areas and departments and you become focused on your part of the task and not who the task is for or the bigger picture. For example, you may create a great deal for new customers to sign up to your product or service, but that could be deemed to be unfair if it is then unavailable to your existing customers. How would you feel about that as an existing customer? In this case, the sales team is focused on acquiring new customers without understanding (or caring about) the impact this has for the retention or service team. You can imagine that if the deal was really good, you might get people phoning your contact centre to get the same deal, or leaving and re-joining to get this deal. The mature audience-centric organisation would invest in an equivalent deal for existing customers.

Audience-centricity, though, is not just at this strategic level, it applies all the way to individual interactions and how you manage these in an audience-centric way.

These are the capabilities that you should be able to deliver against:

- Ensure that the design of interaction strategies match the needs, expectations and desires of individuals, rather than randomly making pre-determined offers to an arbitrarily selected group of people.

- You no longer try to find out which people will buy a certain product, instead you try to understand which products a certain person would be interested in – i.e. matching actions to people, not people to actions.

- The individual's interests (as tracked by their content consumption), maps them to personas and journeys in your audience engagement strategy which then determines the content pillars that you are using for engagement with this person. You engage with each person through content that is not about your products or services, but about a mutual interest area – the point of mutuality which we will discuss later).

- An individual can join an engagement cycle at any point and be able to take their own path through the story. But you will always know where they are in real-time and be able to supply the next best piece of content for their journey.

- It is possible for you to have a two-way conversation with your audience. This may be by surveying regularly to assess the quality of the products or services or it might include Net Promoter Score (NPS, http://www.netpromoter.com/). However, if your business is going to take a truly mature approach to audience-centricity, there is an open 'channel' so that you can constantly assess and understand your audience's needs.

- You review the effect of changes in the business environment on your audience and can update the strategy as appropriate.

Dynamic Interactions

Imagine that you are talking to a friend; this is an old friend so you know their background and interests. You have not seen each other for a couple of weeks so you are catching up. As the conversation goes back and forth, you hear their news, which prompts things you want to say or ask about. You then tell them your news and the same thing happens. You are talking about things that interest the both of you and the conversation moves forward by listening and responding.

In order to be good at 'Dynamic Interactions' you need to be able to manage potentially millions of interactions with your audience in the same way. When you can do this, you create a deeper and more personal relationship with your audience than when you simply follow a 'one size fits all' approach and manage for your process efficiency and not the individual's needs.

Here are some points to consider:

- Your customer's (and we mean customer on this occasion and not audience) inbound experience should be deliberately variable, driven by dynamic 'real-time' assessments of the customer's situation, interests, risks and value. As each successive interchange with the customer may alter the information on which the assessments are based; assessments need to take place in real-time so that the customer perceives that the organisation is responding directly to him or her and making the most personalised, relevant engagement possible. (This is achieved by implementing a real-time Decision Engine.)

- Inbound interaction strategies are designed as a combination of multiple types of business rules and propensity models. The propensity models are not stored separately; they are executed along with the rules in real-time, dependent on the customer's context (process/mood/state). This means they can be executed for any process and will behave differently for each customer. There is no pre-determination of which customer will receive which offer or content provided there is a strategy designed to address the set of circumstances at hand. By managing the interaction this way, it is also possible for multiple offers or messages to be executed during each conversation.

- Outbound interaction strategies are guided by the audience engagement strategy. This will be updated in real-time as to the individual's status so that the next item to be served is aligned to their journey.

Interactive Product/
Service Configurability

Imagine shopping for your groceries in an 'old fashioned' store.
All the vegetables, meats and produce are loose and your shopkeeper
will weigh out the goods you require or you can use the scales
and weigh out some of the produce yourself. There are no fixed
'packages'. Your shopping basket will be completely different to
the next person's. In this example, the products and the service are
completely configurable by you, the customer. In the modern world
though, packages are convenient and fast. In today's world it is more
likely your basket will match the next shopper's and this also makes it
easier for the shopkeeper. There are advantages and disadvantages
to both models. To be mature in this principle, you have to decide the
right balance of this 'configurability' for your products and services.
This should be done, as always, from the customer's point of view and
not what is easiest for you.

Take your insurance policies; most of us have lots of different types of insurance from car, to home, to life. Wouldn't it be a lot easier for that to be bundled together in one package? Couldn't you then get a discount for buying this sort of package? The reality is that this is extremely hard for the insurance companies because of the way that the policies are usually administered in different systems with

different rules for how they decide what your premium is. But the creative marketer could imagine a way that some parts of this could be possible.

If you could configure your products and services the following would be possible:

- Agents will be empowered to interactively negotiate with the customer to configure a proposition that will match the customer's needs.

- Customers can share opinions on products and services with the organisation and see changes as a result of that collaboration.

- Customers can participate interactively in designing products and services.

- The negotiation experience is graduated to use resources – both time and money – exactly where and when they will be most productive. For example, the relationship may

start with a low-key consultation in which the customer simply learns about available products. Over time, as the customer gains confidence and trust in the company's recommendations, advice and understanding of his or her needs, the relationship can become a more mutual one in which the pluses and minuses of different products are discussed. Finally, as requirements are satisfied, the relationship can evolve again into a maintenance mode where contact is made only when required and is styled to be unobtrusive with the promise that the organisation is always there when needed.

As you move to managing an audience by publishing content through your engagement strategy, your publications become part of the service that you are providing them.

As you monitor the success of each piece of content, you can start to configure the stories to address your audience's needs.

Customer Selectivity

Customer selectivity recognises that not all customers are created equal. As a commercial organisation it is just a fact that making investments in some customers pays off in the long-term. This is the ugly truth that some customers are more valuable to you and some will cost you more but not return value to the business. As it is a sensitive area and one where your reputation as a business is at stake, it must be managed carefully. What you must be able to understand about each customer is what their 'Net Present Value' is. How you calculate this and your ability to calculate it will vary depending on the data you have access to and how your products are structured. Basically though, it is the following formula:

SALES
Cost to serve/supply

PREDICTED
future sales

DISCOUNT %

The discount percentage is applied to bring back the future sales numbers to the present day estimation. Whilst this calculation may seem simple enough, in large complex organisations it can prove very elusive. Often you will find that you will be working with a proxy for some of the data and therefore the interactions and solutions that you design must take this into account.

If you have got a formula for this, then solutions can be individualised and interactions guided based on the long-term value of a customer. Advanced capability in this area allows you to calculate it in real-time, during the current interaction.

Then:

- Investments in more or less profitable customers can be increased or decreased accordingly.

- Propositions, customer insight and predictions are adapted both offline and in real-time based on customer responses and information learnt in previous and current interactions.

- Propensity models are refined and regularly updated to keep up with the latest behaviour shown by customers.

- Propensity models can be built in real-time and adapted based on responses and information gathered during customer interactions. These adaptive models modify the underlying process flow on the fly to deliver more appropriate actions.

- A view of all interactions is available to any employee who needs to see them in order to improve the interaction with the customer.

A Note on Audience Selectivity

The inverse is perhaps true when we look at the audience. In some respects your audience is self-selecting, and you will only be engaged with those that you share a point of mutuality with. However, we treat the audience as if they are all created equal. This means that we are not simply focusing on those that respond positively. If you do this, you will create audience 'fatigue'. By following a story map you take the whole audience with you and more importantly you do not start to 'leak' prospects from your funnel.

Holistic & Actionable Customer View

This principle is all about your data. It started life in the CRM world as 'single customer view' and many CRM projects delivered successfully on this principle. Very often, single customer view meant one physical database where all the data from various systems was gathered together. The problem with this approach is that the data was then not necessarily suitable for the different applications and may not have even been useful or actionable. For example, statistical data mining requires the data in a particular format, so statisticians would extract the data they wanted and 'flatten it' for their purposes. However, this requires a lot of effort every time you want to build a predictive model. Campaign management/database marketing tools then require a different set of data in a different format. The reality very quickly becomes apparent that one database and physical structure cannot serve all these needs. The result is that you then end up with several different stores and various mechanisms to keep them all aligned.

Now there is a new challenge: 'Big Data'. How does that fit with what you have got already and how you move forward? As with customers, not all data is created equal and it should serve a purpose and improve your engagement with a customer in order to be of value. This is why this principle has moved from a 'single customer view' to 'holistic and actionable'. Holistic means that it has everything it needs about customers in a way that suits each application. Actionable means that you are not storing data that you are unable to do anything with. For example, your customer's eye colour is most probably completely irrelevant if you are a bank. That might seem obvious, but you will probably find data that you can do nothing with, it just takes up space and costs you money to maintain it.

The following points outline the areas to consider when getting your data built:

- Data is structured around customer attributes to provide a holistic view of an individual customer, including products owned, personal information, recent conversations and proposition responses.

- Data is not structured around products or processes – you do not need to know how many of process 'A' have been performed on product 'B'.

- The data is available where it needs to be actioned to make recommendations and improve engagement (within any channel).

- Relevant customer information can be accessed by employees from any department or functional area, regardless of which department or functional area collected it.

- The content 'trail' is maintained for each person. Each piece of content that your individual audience member consumes adds details to their profile about their interests and where they are on their content journey.

Consistency & Unification

In order to achieve maturity in the consistency and unification principle you need to deliver all communications against an over-arching marketing strategy. Seems logical and sensible enough, but very often there is no marketing strategy that is cascaded amongst the marketing team as their objectives. It is about organisation and process as much as it is about the technologies and methodologies to deliver. If, as a team, you are not all pointing in the same direction, you cannot expect that your communications will be consistent to your audience. Very often this happens in large marketing departments where everyone is focused on their channel, campaign or product and they are not unified around the audience. In more advanced marketing departments you will at least see teams organised around customer segments.

Within the marketing strategy should be an audience engagement strategy. This will determine who you are talking to about what, when and through what channels. It is the audience engagement strategy that will increase engagement with your audience by making your communications consistent. The audience engagement strategy is created and managed through an Engagement Strategy Planner (ESP). (This doesn't currently exist as a piece of technology, but it is coming soon.)

Technology can help in this principle by providing a Decision Engine capability for inbound interaction and campaign management tools for outbound interactions. These should then be integrated through the ESP as the overarching 'brain' that controls your communications. If you have this capability you will be able to achieve the following:

- Every communication, decision or offer in every channel is guided by a centralised editorial authority that is both technological and organisational.

- Inbound and outbound channels are co-ordinated via the ESP so there is no inconsistency of communication with the target audience.

- Experiences are unified and the relationship spans all channels and processes that affect the audience. Whether a self-service, agent-assisted or back-office process that changes some aspect of the relationship, all need to be unified and transparent, so an interaction that began in one channel can be viewed and completed seamlessly in another.

- The ESP can unify the organisation so that what the business is doing and planning is fed into marketing and also how the audience is feeling and reacting is fed back into the business.

Process Orchestration

This principle is not just about the marketing functions, it is about making sure that as the audience transitions through different parts of your organisation that this is not apparent to them; the experience that they receive should be consistent. As a marketer, it is important to understand that internal marketing is required to deliver on your plans. If the rest of the organisation is unaware of your strategies then you cannot expect them to behave consistently in the delivery of your messages. If you create a proposition that will get the audience to call your contact centre and you have not told the contact centre about it, what do you think will happen? All engagement cycles should have a process flow that maps the entire experience for the audience. That means understanding this all the way through to your back-office and not just to the point of sale where you would think that the marketing job ends. If you are an online retailer for example, how and when will the customer get the product that they have ordered? Is this consistent with what you have told the customer at the point of sale?

To do this well…

- Front-office decisions are tied to back-office processes to ensure end-to-end management and a seamless experience for employees and the audience.

- Workflow and enterprise case management tools are in place to automate, orchestrate and optimise case, task, or work management from the point of origination through to the point of completion.

- Specifically within marketing, the organisation and processes that you put in place to manage the audience engagement strategy will be your focus. It should go without saying that these should be efficient and streamlined, but if you do not reorganise as if you were a publisher then your organisation will not behave with the right mentality and this will just block up the publishing flow. Look to the national papers and how they are organised around editors and sub-editors who have final say in order to maintain quality, but also a very straight line to maintain speed and volume.

Relationship Management

Relationship management means having a relentless focus on the customer. Customers should be viewed as assets and their relationships with the organisation should be planned to maximise the value of those assets. Planning should encompass all types of relationship the enterprise offers, such as those for the new customer, the confident customer and the mature customer. Planning must consider the choice and order of presenting propositions through the stages of the relationship including the sequencing of outbound communications to stimulate contact, inbound contacts to enact the relationship and outbound communications again to solidify those contacts. By simulating customer changes and differing decisions, different scenarios can be explored, strategies chosen and targets set.

These are the things that you should look to achieve:

- Holistic engagement strategy plans that transcend silos and channels and are designed to maximise the relationship and bottom line.

- Inbound and outbound channels join in cross-functional collaboration to design and manage strategic customer/content marketing plans.

- Customer information is integrated across various functions that interact with the customer such as sales, marketing and customer service.

- Customer relationships are treated as a valuable asset.

- Senior management emphasises the importance of customer relationships.

- Customers trust that the organisation will talk to them about the right offers for them.

- The roles of sales and service may be combined.

- Each experience is appropriate. Odd as it may seem, the relationship or interaction with the customer does not need to be the most complete relationship or interaction possible. Rather, it is the right experience for the right individual at a particular point in time. Offer incentives only to those who require them. Spend time only with those who will be influenced by your attention.

Command & Control

This is about being able to see and understand how all your communications are performing and being able to make adjustments accordingly. Ideally, you should be able to do this in real-time for all your digital channels and your contact centres. In order to deliver on this you must have 'closed-loop' marketing. What this means is that for everything you communicate you know what the results are with everyone that is sent it, receives it or reads it. Campaign management technology has evolved such that it is possible to trace all your outbound communications. Decision Engines can do the same for your inbound channels. You need to understand what did not work as much as what has worked.

Every communication, the audience's subsequent behaviour, and the economic implications and impact on resources this behaviour has, must be captured. Individually, this data forms the basis for future interactions with that target audience. Collectively monitoring like this forms the basis for reporting on the performance and compliance of the propositions you are offering as well as the logic and processes it is using to do so. This provides the basis for simulating the implications of changes in the target audience base, and of the impact of regulatory events and competitive actions.

As you get this monitoring in place and are able to align your campaigns to your engagement strategy, you can transition the campaigns to sustained engagement and not simply 'one-off' campaigns. This will in turn change your marketing activities to focus on audience engagement as opposed to bombarding your prospects and customers.

From a technology perspective this is where we need to use a number of solutions:

- The ESP would be used to plan and map the audience engagement strategy, then to manage the delivery and execution. It will also allow you to monitor all the activity in real-time so that you can make adjustments to the plan as described below.

- Campaign management tools will report on each campaign through the definition of the response model.

- For 'inbound' monitoring, a Decision Engine is appropriate.

Ideally, this type of capability will enable you to simulate different scenarios to test what the optimum balance is between your various communications and channels. Through this simulation you see all the various propositions that are controlled by parameters, rules and models and adjust the thresholds on all of them, replaying all the decisions that had been made up to the current moment. You would then be able to see what impact it would have on the bottom line if you had made different decisions. This would offer some estimate of what the future may hold, but it is not an exact science. This is not just campaign optimisation, but total engagement optimisation that allows you to 're-run' the past with new content until you get the best possible outcome overall rather than for just one campaign or a series of campaigns. Once you have a new audience engagement strategy that you believe will give optimal results, the management tool should allow you to commit the changes instantly, so they will be in place for the next communication.

The ideal system must enable you to continuously control the audience experience and balance that experience with organisational objectives. Whether to alter the experience to cope with excessive call centre queues, stock outs or over commitments, or to keep the level and quality of experience the same, decisions need to be controlled. Parameters must be embedded into the communication logic to provide flexibility, allowing messages to be switched on or off, levels of activity, such as offers or interventions, to be moved up or down, and process paths to be changed based on real-time monitoring of the current situation and future projections.

In this chapter

- Maturity Model
  Structure & Levels

Maturity Model

PART II: Model Structure & Levels

As we said at the beginning of this section, the principles are business behaviours, practices and capabilities that when put in place properly will significantly improve the organisation's bottom line. We are now ready to see how the principles come together to form the model. The purpose of creating a model from these principles is to create a benchmark and a measurement for where you are. Once you have an accurate view of your current position it is much easier to plan your roadmap to improve. Measurement of maturity against this best practice is determined by five levels, with level five being the highest. Whilst there is a score for each principle and each dimension, you do not have to have a perfect score on everything to reach a level five – as a business it is not practical to have a perfect score. Instead, it is best to balance implementing certain capabilities against your business model, size and requirements. As we will discuss in business outcomes, the case for any capability implementation is unique to your business. Also, do not assume that you need to achieve a level five in your business at all. It has to be what is appropriate to the levels of engagement that will improve the KPIs for your business.

The model can be used as a benchmark for assessing where you are and identifying where you will get the best bang for your buck by implementing certain capabilities or changing the way that you operate.

ICE Maturity Model

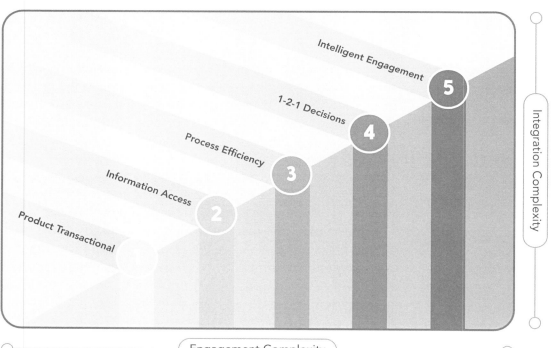

Dimensions

The model is based on two primary dimensions – engagement complexity and integration complexity. Maturity is measured in each of the principles and the dimensions to then give an overall maturity level for an organisation.

- **Engagement complexity** at level 4 and above is defined as the capability to have 'one-to-one' conversations with your target audience. These conversations may span time and channels, but the key to making them unique is that they must adapt in real-time, based on audience responses and status – the end result being intelligent and managed dialogues. This capability is not only important in a service or sales situation, but in any process where the organisation is looking for an optimal outcome for both parties to enhance the relationship. Many organisations have focused their efforts at the point past the first sale. By implementing technology that can make the appropriate prompts we can enhance cross-sell/up-sell and retention capabilities. However, a fully engaged audience is both before the first sale and beyond the last sale or service. Engagement complexity at levels 4 and 5 is about managing your entire funnel and not the prospective customers who have just arrived at your door.

- **Integration complexity** is not simply about technical integration but also refers to the organisation's ability to integrate around the audience. From a technical standpoint, at level 4 there would be an operational single audience view. Strategies that are executed with audiences using this view are designed for multiple channels by multiple lines of business and functions within the organisation but they are managed centrally via an Engagement Strategy Plan. This controls all inbound and outbound communications. Decisions and actions taken within the front-office are coordinated with the back-office processes. The audience relationships are considered to be a valuable asset and the rules that govern decisions made whilst communicating with the audiences reflect that.

The principles relate to the model dimensions as follows:

Engagement Complexity	Integration Complexity
Individuality	Holistic & Actionable Customer View
Customer-Centricity	Consistency & Unification
Dynamic Interactions	Process Orchestration
Product Configuration	Relationship Management
Customer Selectivity	Command & Control

Before discussing the level definitions you may have seen if you've looked at the benchmark section, most organisations score at level 3. This benchmark research is predominantly for B2C organisations that have millions of customers. As such, the capabilities descriptions and progression through the levels is described for these sorts of organisations. For smaller organisations and B2B organisations it is a matter of scaling appropriately and finding the appropriate techniques that deliver the results for your business model. The principles are, however, the same. Given level 3 is where most organisations find themselves, we have focused more on moving from level 3 to levels 4 and 5 than the other levels.

Level Definitions
Level 1 - Product Transactional

In organisations that score at level 1, of which there are still some, customer-facing processes are usually not automated or related to customer engagement. This, however, may well be appropriate for the business model. For example, where the product is a commodity, there may be no commercial reason to invest in relationships with customers. As such, there would be no stable environment for managing customers, just an array of different product management systems.

Success in organisations that have not matured (and do need to manage relationships) depends on the effort level of the people in the organisation. At this level, the firm will be organised around products and processes rather than customers. Employee performance will be measured in relation to how many products they sell or processes they complete rather than how well they serve the customer. There is very little planning, executive buy-in, or coordination for customer management. Understanding the requirement for customer engagement is limited.

Lack of strategy and management causes:

- Over or under-communication with customers; lack of individual treatment; message repetition.

- Poor crisis management and an inability to repeat past successes.

The capability components that we would expect to be in place for an organisation at level 1 may be just a series of 'back-office' or 'legacy' systems that support product or order processing. These systems can be very complex and difficult to maintain. Data is organised around product attributes rather than customer attributes. Processing may be consolidated into a single desktop for contact centre purposes, but in some cases there is no 'front-office'.

The Intelligent Marketing Institute

Moving From Level 1 to Level 2

Progression from any level to the next will mean implementing both organisational and technical changes. These changes will give the organisation new capabilities.

If the organisation could benefit from a customer-led approach then firstly you need to gain insight into customer behaviour that allows the development of new business strategies. Not all organisations do need to change, and in some cases a customer-centric business approach is not appropriate. However, if you are making this change, we suggest that the following items may need to be implemented:

- A view of customer data, at least in an off-line or reporting data warehouse.

- Data that is structured around customer attributes, not product or process attributes.

- Reporting and MI from a customer perspective.

Then you need systems and processes that allow you to treat customers as customers, not as processes or products. To create and deliver targeted communications to customers we suggest the following:

- Campaign management

- Segmentation methodologies

- Campaign & channel strategy

In looking at how to approach implementing all these various capabilities, it does not have to be all done in-house. It is possible to outsource any and all of these capabilities rather than build them yourselves and it will depend on what resources and capabilities you already have as to which is the appropriate route for you.

Level 2 - Information Access

In organisations that score at level 2, processes are simple and focused on order management and complaint management (servicing); however, basic CRM capabilities do not exist. Any customer information that you have may be held off-line and presented to the agents for information only. A data warehouse may be in place, but is just for reporting purposes and some basic campaigning. Some customer analytics are in place, but insight is not actionable except for crude campaign targeting. Furthermore, channels are not coordinated with common messages between them and marketing activities are not coordinated with service or contact centres. Contact centres may be in silos by types of process or segments of customers.

The capabilities that we would expect to be in place for an organisation at level 2 are:

- There may be a series of 'back-office' or 'legacy' systems that support product or order processing. These systems can be very complex and difficult to maintain.

- Data is organised by product rather than by customer in the front-office. A warehouse or other data source exists to consolidate the customer data, which can then be used for analysis and reporting.

- Processing may be consolidated to a single desktop for contact centre purposes.

- Campaign management is in place as a function and as a technical application. However, we would not expect it to manage campaigns across multiple channels. In fact, campaigns will probably be targeted to product response segments rather than to customer segments.

- Some middleware is in place to consolidate the data from the various product processing platforms into a customer view.

- Customer data is not available to the front-office for update, but it may be available to query.

The Intelligent Marketing Institute

Moving From Level 2 to Level 3

At level 2, the organisation now has customer data, but it is in an off-line location. This could be a data warehouse or database associated to a campaign management tool, but it is not available to manage the relationship with the customer when they are in contact with you. The next step is to make that data available to the 'front-office', when the customer is in contact with you in any channel. This is usually achieved by implementing a CRM platform.

Implementing a CRM platform will mean changing your processes so that they are customer-focused and moving the off-line data into the CRM platform. You need systems and processes that allow you to treat customers as customers, not as processes or products. That is far from straightforward and is why a lot of organisations have spent many millions doing it.

In order to make the most of your CRM platform there are a number of other capabilities that can be implemented at the same time:

- Segmentation methodologies enhanced with predictive analytics. This will give you the ability to differentiate treatments for customer segments during operational processes.

- Contact & channel strategy development.

- Customer journey mapping.

- Analytical model factory.

- Campaign management tools.

- Tying front-office decisions to back-office processes and incorporating workflow management to ensure seamless end-to-end processes.

- Integration of systems and the organisation around customers.

- Skills routing – within the contact centre – calls can be routed according to agent skills.

- Multi-channel/multi-line of business contact history that can be accessed by any authorised user to review customer interactions and ensure consistent treatment.

Level 3 - Process Efficiency

At level 3 you will have now implemented a CRM platform. This should mean that data has been organised around customers as opposed to products and that processes have been redesigned similarly. The success of the CRM implementation will determine how much of this has been achieved and the implementation of a CRM platform should make for better interactions with customers. However, the challenge is that whilst the customer data is front and centre, usually analytical insight is not yet in place to determine the needs and desires of each customer with the ability to then apply that to interactions with the relevant, engaging offer or content. Consequently, there is nothing that supports the 'R' in CRM – i.e. the 'relationship'.

What you will find in an organisation at level 3 is:

- Process complexity is high and there is an operational Customer Relationship Management (CRM) function.

- The single customer view is operational in all channels.

- Contact centres focus on efficiency and repeatability of their processes; consequently interaction complexity is low.

- The goal of the interaction is efficiency rather than profitability or engagement.

- There is little use of analytics to provide any offer management or 'next-best-action'. (For more information on 'next-best-action' please see the chapter on Decision Engines.)

- Outbound campaigns are not coordinated and connected to the inbound activity from customers.

- Campaign management may exist and use segmentation for targeting.

- Processing is consolidated to a single desktop for contact centre purposes.

- Campaign management is in place as a function and as a technical application. However, we would not expect it to manage campaigns across multiple channels. In fact, it will probably be targeted to product response segments rather than to customer segments.

- Middleware is in place to consolidate the data from the various product processing platforms into a single customer view.

Moving From Level 3 to Level 4

Moving from level 3 to level 4 is about implementing a Decision Engine so that customer insight and analytics can be used in each interaction. This means that the interaction complexity increases as each one is tailored to the individual customer's needs. There are many tools that describe themselves as Decision Engine or personalisation tools; however, they do not all have the same level of functionality or sophistication. In section 4 we have defined both the different types of tools that are available and what they do on a spectrum of complexity. As this is a fast-moving area with new tools coming on the market all the time, you will find updates on our online resources. Whilst a less sophisticated tool may not be a full Decision Engine, it does not mean that it is not suitable for your business requirements.

At level 4, the changes are at the interaction level. Each experience can be tailored to the individual and is perceived as such by the recipient. This is not simply an agent greeting the customer by name. It requires that the needs and objectives of the individual within the current interaction, as well their history and past interactions, govern the flow of the conversation, the actions taken, the content presented and the offers made. By leveraging large amounts of known customer data from multiple sources, applying predictive insight, and bringing the resulting decisions accurately into play through logical interpretation at the point of interaction, each customer can be treated as a 'segment of one' with all aspects of the experience based on that individual. Remember, at level 3 we focused on process efficiency, which meant that there was more of a one-size-fits-all approach to interactions with customers. Not all processes should be changed; there are some things that are best left the same for everyone as this provides consistency for the customers and efficiency for the organisation. For example, if changing payment method from cheque to direct debit, there are not any variances in the way that this should work from one customer to another.

But for other processes the customer's experience should be deliberately variable, driven by dynamic 'just-in-time' assessments of the customer's situation, interests, risks and value. As each successive interchange with the customer may alter the information on which the assessments are based, assessments need to take place in real-time so the customer perceives that the organisation is responding directly to him or her and making the most personalised, relevant decision possible. It should be like having a real human conversation – one-to-one, not one-to-many.

CASE STUDY

O2 is an example of a business that moved from level 2 to level 4 through the implementation of a Decision Engine. The reason that this was a move from level 2 is due to the fact that no CRM system was in place when the project started, there were only a series of platforms that took care of the billing processes. O2 was one of the first organisations to implement a Decision Engine to manage customer relationships more effectively. Many more organisations have since adopted this approach. It was the first project of its kind and was ground-breaking at the time. Once implemented, O2 was able to tailor its services to individual customer profiles rather than grouping them into generic customer sets based on factors such as age, sex, occupation and monthly spending bands. When the project began, the company had a large department of analysts carrying out project-based analysis of their customers in order to create specific segments and targeting models. This approach was too slow and did not deliver actionable results immediately. Rather than making predictions, they were simply 'slicing and dicing' the data. Very traditional outbound marketing campaigns were carried out and as the target ROI was much larger than the number of people from each segment, more people were targeted than necessary. The first task was to organise the customer data into a manageable form which then allowed the generation of intelligence. This enabled the production of large volumes of predictions very quickly. To begin with this was used primarily for outbound campaigns, which saw a greater response rate than previously as they were far more accurately targeted.

A Real-Time Environment

The next step was to build and implement the real-time decision environment. O2 branded the project 'Vision' and this became the name of the application that was used in the contact centres. Vision concentrates all of the intelligence and actions involved in talking to a customer and links to all other applications in order to fulfil this. The real-time environment is key, as in order to create the most relevant dialogue it needs to be based upon the current data held on the customer. Vision also has a record of where the conversation ended so that customers are not made the same offer twice. This can then be made available across all channels, which means that wherever the customer contacts the company there is a 'memory' of what happened most recently.

O2 also has a real-time monitoring application that gives a minute-by-minute update of the trading situation, daily, weekly and monthly reporting, as well as the ability to interrogate the data produced with the mining tool to get more 'insight' in to what is working and what is not. This gives ultimate control over how the business is run.

Success

The results of the customer experience implementation at O2 speak for themselves. O2 has seen its success rate of fewer than 2% conversion rate increase to over 70% with the implementation of the Decision Engine. Return on investment is significant. Closed loop reporting indicates 9% average revenue per user (ARPU) uplift, not including churn benefit and customer experience measures. O2 also abandoned its average handling time measures in the call centre and there has been a move to quality over quantity. The prediction process now takes a seventh of the time it used to.

NOTE:

These results were achieved at the beginning of the project; as was proved with other companies and projects, over time these results decrease. The reason is that within an overall customer pool only a certain number of customers will contact the company on an inbound call and do that reasonably regularly. Over time, the company runs out of things to say and also 'wears out' these customers. You get audience fatigue. For example, you want to move customers to pay by direct debit. At the beginning you may have a 70% conversion rate to do that. But further on you have converted everyone who is going to convert and therefore your conversion rate drops. The challenge that these organisations face is how to get the audience re-engaged so that they start calling in again and feed the Decision Engine beast. That is what ICE is about.

The Intelligent Marketing Institute

Creating a relationship between an individual customer and a large corporation, or even between companies, can be very challenging if not impossible. Getting more data about how your customers behave will mean that you can readdress the fundamentals such as targeting. Once real-time decisions are truly embed within the organisation you can target your offers based on the relationship that the customer has with you as a company and not how they interact with your product or your publications.

By embracing the benefits that these intelligent processes can bring, O2 is able to treat the customer as an individual with personalised, human-like conversations and relevant and timely offers. O2's customer relationships are continuing to grow and this is only possible because technology is playing such a crucial role.

Level 4 – One-to-One Decisions

Organisations that have scored at level 4 are able to intelligently engage their audience on a one-to-one basis. Every interaction will be personalised to the recipient and the goal of each interaction is engagement. A more engaged audience leads to more profitable customers.

An organisation that is at level 4 will have usually implemented a Decision Engine as described above. The indicators that the organisation is at this level are:

- Process and interaction complexity is high.

- The goal of the interaction is engagement rather than efficiency.

- Each process is tailored to individual customer's needs; agents may not follow specific processes.

- Processes are controlled by a high level of analytics and real-time decisions on the analytics.

- A level 4 organisation would have the ability to manage personalised communications in at least one channel from a centralised Decision Engine/authority.

- The rules that the Decision Engine executes are written, designed and maintained via a cross-functional strategy development group using a tool designed for that purpose. This function is centralised across all customer segments and product areas.

Moving From Level 4 to Level 5

You would think that having implemented a Decision Engine, a campaign management tool, predictive mining and a CRM platform that you have done all you can to maximise your relationships with your customers. However, the one thing not yet achieved is integration between your Decision Engine (inbound) and your campaign management tool (outbound).

As you look to improve your engagement with customers, integration of these two capabilities will be a key factor. It may surprise you to read that no one has successfully integrated an inbound Decision Engine tool with an outbound campaign management tool. Whilst it might be possible technically to crack that nut, it will never work if you do not step back and understand that each capability has a context within the customer's journey that affects how it works.

To explain this better, let's frame each tool and how they are used:

Mostly, Decision Engines are used in channels where the customer is contacting the company (inbound). Again, mostly this is via contact centres but some organisations have done this in their websites. What it does is analyse the data for the customer who has just turned up and predict, with the help of statistical models, what they will most likely say yes to from all the possible propositions the organisation has and then present that to them – assuming that the rules are set this way; some companies put a revenue override on this so that the most profitable item is prioritised. It might not be a sale that is proposed so it is sometimes known as next-best-action. There is some debate about what qualifies as real-time, but for the purpose of this discussion it is about using the customer's current context or stated intent in the calculations as to what to offer them. Effectively this can be giving them what they asked for, but it is slightly more complicated than that. The primary prediction is if they will buy the product or say yes. There may be others but this is the main type of model used.

Campaign management tools take the opposite approach in a number of ways.

Firstly, it is an outbound communication with the company sending a message to multiple customers. Secondly, most campaigns pick the proposition that they are promoting and then find all the customers that might say yes to this or 'respond'. Where the Decision Engine only works for one customer at a time in real-time, campaign management is one message for groups or segments of customers and is not real-time – real-time marketing solutions, as opposed to real-time decisioning tools, are presenting a predetermined message in real-time but not calculating it in real-time. The primary model is a response model, this means the likelihood they will **respond** to the campaign. This is not necessarily the same as will they buy the product, although sometimes both are used.

The integration premise goes that you should be able to use the rules, statistical models and code of the Decision Engine to personalise each instance of the campaign as it goes out. That is technically challenging as it requires an awful lot of processing power to run thousands if not millions of predictions in order to execute the campaign. This can mean that the processing window may be extremely long, to the point where the first customers processed may have called into your contact centre in the meantime so their status has changed. This would mean a misfired communication in the campaign at best. An added challenge is that there is no context for the Decision Engine, in other words the real-time data that it would use on the inbound channel. The drive to try and make this integration work is strong, though, as the results of inbound Decision Engines are significantly better, on the face of it, than outbound campaigns. The theory is that the predictive accuracy of the Decision Engine is the contributing factor to the success and that if you could add this to outbound campaigns you would get the same results.

But 'what-if' prediction is not the only thing that makes it work so well? What if it is also customer context and the fact that they have come to you? Of course, saying the right thing and making the right offer when they turn up is important and does have significant impact. And this is not to say that personalisation in outbound communications does not have an impact, it does, but to go to the level that a Decision Engine can achieve will not bring you the results that you expect.

This is because it is more about where the customer is in their journey. What this means is that Decision Engines are good when the customer is already engaged. They are effectively at the bottom of the funnel which is the final act of the journey. By measuring the Decision Engine in isolation, it gets all the glory for the sale or conversion when in fact the engagement path may have involved a lot of other communication that has contributed to the customer being receptive to the offer in the first place.

But the type of model used also has an impact. President Barack Obama's 2012 re-election campaign was able to successfully utilise data analytics to help turn out voters. The analytical team used an 'uplift' model to precisely identify voters who were leaning toward Republican Mitt Romney, but were likely to be receptive to the Obama campaign's message.

Uplift modelling is all about finding the 'persuadable'. In any group of voters, or potential customers, some people have already decided; in marketing terms, they plan to buy your product even if you do not advertise to them, or they are dead set against doing so. For those who have already decided, your Decision Engine still counts these as a win when they turn up and say yes. Another set of people are likely to be turned off if they are contacted; they should also be left alone. But then there are those who need some convincing and are open to being convinced. The Obama analysts built, tested and refined a set of predictive models in an effort to statistically identify the characteristics of persuadable voters in swing states. The Obama campaign then used the models to optimise online and TV ad buys and to determine which doors canvassers should knock on, which voters should be called and which ones should receive mailings. The success of the re-election campaign is some proof that uplift modelling works. The uplift modelling approach enables marketers to focus campaigns more efficiently, and potentially increase sales in the process, by targeting 'persuadable' consumers.

There are some trade-offs and complications to be aware of. The cost per conversion typically increases with uplift modelling because 'sure-thing customers' are no longer counted towards the conversion number, which they are by the Decision Engine method. There is also the cost of the analytical work required to determine the characteristics of persuadable customers and identify the people who fit that profile. If it is done correctly you can do more with less outbound communications.

Measuring the Right Things

What you really should be thinking about is engagement, not response. Instead of modelling response or purchase we need to analyse the 'journey' and find the audience that will buy **only** if they get some more content (persuasion). Ideally, we are finding the next-best piece of content for this person that takes them toward the goal for their persona.

So rather than trying to apply a one-size-fits-all approach and make the Decision Engine

the overriding central 'brain' controlling all communications, it is far better to use an audience engagement strategy to manage the customer's whole journey. A 'horses for courses' approach is more effective. In this context, the campaign management tool's job is to move the customer along this path towards the Decision Engine, not to close the deal. It then becomes a matter of understanding what the business outcomes are for each capability and not having the same expectations for inbound and outbound. Simply put, the customer is in a different place outbound, they require a bit more convincing. If campaigns are delivered in line with an engagement strategy this then helps 'feed' the Decision Engine with customers ready to convert. Each tool has a part to play in different parts of the customer's engagement cycle/journey.

Level 5 – Intelligent Engagement

The difference between levels 4 and 5 is the ability to execute your strategies consistently omni-channel and to be able to see and control all those interactions from a central dashboard reporting/engagement strategy capability. Essentially, you will have created a command centre for your business.

The key to achieving this is to align the audience engagement strategy, channel strategy, campaign management capabilities and Decision Engine capabilities through the Engagement Strategy Planner.

These are the characteristics of an organisation at level 5:

- Process complexity is high and interaction complexity is high.

- The goal of the interaction is engagement rather than efficiency.

- All interactions in all channels are controlled by a central dashboard and decision authority.

- Each process is tailored to an individual customer's needs'.

- Visibility and control of all interactions and the inter-relationship between them is managed in real-time.

- The ESP will show a complete view of the entire audience and interactions with that audience across all channels with the ability to slice, dice and drill down on any detail. It would also be possible to try out 'what-if' scenarios to view the impact of certain propositions or proposition changes on the business.

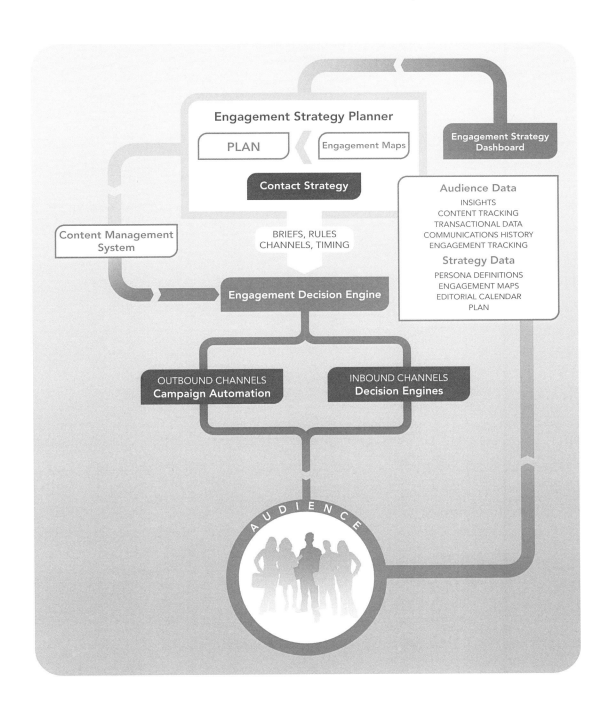

Engagement Strategy Planner

PLAN < Engagement Maps

Engagement Strategy Dashboard

Contact Strategy

Content Management System

BRIEFS, RULES
CHANNELS, TIMING

Audience Data
INSIGHTS
CONTENT TRACKING
TRANSACTIONAL DATA
COMMUNICATIONS HISTORY
ENGAGEMENT TRACKING

Strategy Data
PERSONA DEFINITIONS
ENGAGEMENT MAPS
EDITORIAL CALENDAR
PLAN

Engagement Decision Engine

OUTBOUND CHANNELS
Campaign Automation

INBOUND CHANNELS
Decision Engines

AUDIENCE

Maturity Model
PART III: The Benchmark

We felt it useful to relate this model to existing data on customer engagement that was based on the same methodology around principles and levels. That research looked at 450 companies across seven industry sectors and 12 countries (there were two respondents per company). The results from the survey provided valuable benchmark data for any organisation wishing to understand their position among their peers and is comparable to the levels that we have defined within our maturity level.

The survey consisted of 93 questions based on the 10 principles, which were targeted at heads of marketing, sales, customer service and CRM in the following industries: retail, retail banking, insurance, high-tech, telecommunications, hotels, car rental agencies, energy & utilities, central government and airlines. The interviews were carried out in the following countries: Austria, Belgium, Germany, Luxembourg, Netherlands, Norway, Poland, Spain, and the United Kingdom.

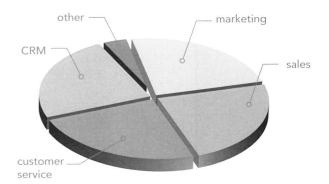

The findings were extremely telling, with 3% of companies benchmarking at level 1; 22% at level 2; 51% at level 3; 24% at level 4; and none achieving a level 5 placement. This distribution was largely in line with

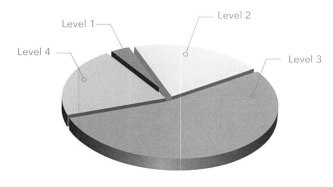

Level 1 — Level 2

Level 4 —

— Level 3

expectations, as levels 1-3 cover traditional CRM capabilities. The vast majority of the companies surveyed had succeeded in achieving a respectable level of process efficiency in their customer-facing operations. This corresponds with principle 8: Process

Orchestration. Using CRM technologies to integrate the front-end with back-office systems, these companies had streamlined interactions with customers, tying front and back-end processes together to achieve a more or less seamless process management flow. Front-to-back integration also provides a more comprehensive view of the customer, giving employees access to all the data they would need to respond appropriately to basic customer inquiries. At this level, the goal of interaction is efficiency, with the hope of completing the customer interaction in a single phone call. On the other hand, virtually all of the industries performed badly in principle 4: The Ability to Negotiate With Customers in Real-Time.

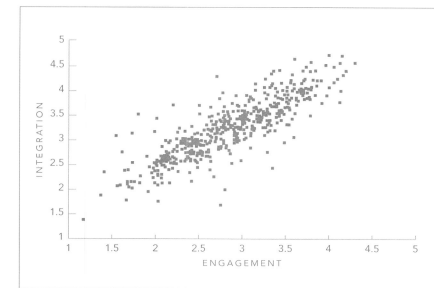

If we take a look at where all the companies were placed on the model, we can see that there was a strong grouping along a diagonal line across the model. This indicates that there is a strong correlation between integration and engagement. For an organisation to improve their engagement they need to be more integrated.

The Intelligent Marketing Institute

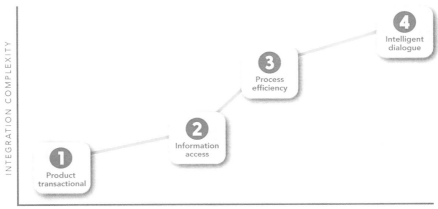

There is further validation of this when we do a 'cluster' analysis to see where companies are grouped. Firstly, this shows us that the level definitions are valid in that there are five main clusters. What is interesting is that there is a steep jump on the integration dimension from levels 2 to 3. This is where we see traditional CRM solutions have been implemented and an organisation has made a shift in managing its processes around customers rather than products.

However, the data starts to get more interesting when we look at performance on a company-by-company basis. The companies rate their performance in terms of market share, retention, profitability, and customer satisfaction. What emerged as we correlated individual maturity scores was that overall, the higher the company's maturity level, the higher their performance in these areas.

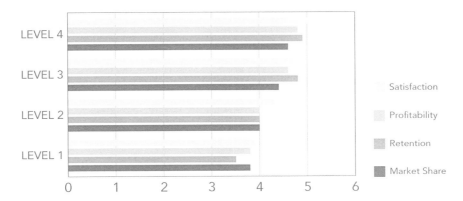

Customer Satisfaction

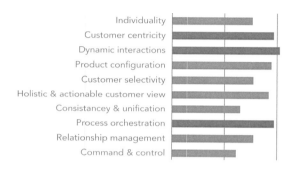

Retention

Profitability

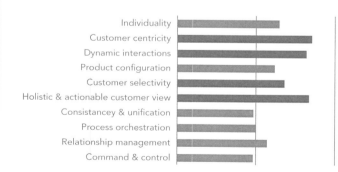

Market Share

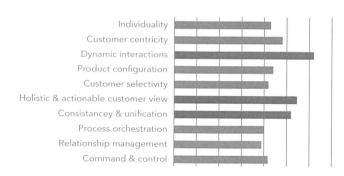

By then correlating the scores of each company to the 10 principles, it becomes possible to see how the principles impact a company's performance. All the principles have a strong correlation to the success factors, but we are able to determine which of the 10 principles have more impact.

Interestingly, Dynamic Interaction was highly correlated in all of the success factors. This capability is perhaps truly where the 'rubber meets the road' in terms of relating to your customers on a one-to-one level, responding appropriately and effectively to their needs and desires in real-time, and maintaining some sense of a conversation, thus creating engagement.

Overall, the findings are directly in line with the original hypothesis, that improving customer engagement will deliver significant economic benefits to the companies that are committed to doing so.

A Note on Maturity and Net Promoter Score

The Net Promoter Score is a discipline by which companies profitably grow by focusing on their customers. It is a key metric for an organisation to understand how it is creating customer value – more at www.netpromoter.com. For organisations looking at how to improve in audience engagement and increase their maturity score in this model, Net Promoter would be a measure that would fit with the 'Customer Selectivity' principle. A successful ICE programme would include many of the same initiatives that are suggested for a successful Net Promoter programme. However, ICE maturity looks in more detail at how audience engagement is first created and then managed.

In this chapter

- Tips on Approach

Tips for Success

The model has described all the various capabilities that make for a fully audience-centric and audience-engaged organisation. But it does not tell you how to go about implementing it. The approach to take will vary based on your business model and where you are starting from. However, the following points are some 'hints & tips' that should give you a guide as to what to look out for and how to get started. We provide a more detailed implementation and staging plan in section 4.

As you will have gathered by now, implementing an audience engagement strategy is not simply a new tactic that can be introduced in isolation. This is an approach which, if implemented to its fullest and most mature extent, stretches across vast swathes of the organisation. It therefore has ramifications, both structurally and diplomatically, that make planning 'how you are going to do it' almost as important as planning 'what you are going to do'. And if you are still in any doubt as to 'why you are going to do it' then rest assured that section 5 covers this.

The principal challenge you will encounter will be regarding who owns the audience within your company. Typically the answer is 'no one', with everyone instead focusing on their own specific engagement channel. This is the result of a disconnected silo state within your organisation and will govern the approach you will have to take when implementing your audience engagement strategy. It also throws up one of the many other challenges you will face, namely the proliferation of content strategies within your business.

So, fundamentally, the approach you will need to adopt will be about taking your internal audience on a journey. From a starting point of product and services silos, your goal will be to create a truly audience-centric organisation, culturally and structurally.

Start With a Trial

TIP 1

The well-trodden path of identifying a way to trial a new approach is by far and away the best place to begin. By doing so, you will be able to accurately measure the impact within a controlled test audience or product/service category. However, more importantly you will be able to engage with all of the key stakeholders within your organisation in a manner that is least likely to threaten or intimidate. This will then allow you to take them on their own journey where they understand how the move to an audience engagement strategy impacts and benefits them.

By running a trial, you will also be developing the full set of processes and structures that will be required for a full rollout – more on this in section 4. However, to do so effectively you will need to not simply identify a specific audience or product/service, but to also ensure that the audience is isolated from other targeted contact and engagement activities. For that reason, it is preferable to be using a specific audience rather than a product or service for the test; if it was the latter, then the target audience would also be bombarded by other marketing initiatives.

It is, however, worth noting that running a trial only accelerates the amount of time it will take to go live by a modest amount. There are no shortcuts to the development of an audience engagement strategy. As such, be mindful of the need to set expectations among those who you need on side and this includes the ability to identify what the positive impact will be. You should also be aware that just because it's a trial does not mean that the systems, processes, and levels of software automation will not be required.

Plan, Plan, Plan

TIP 2

As already emphasised, the weakness of most content strategies is that very little strategic planning is undertaken and the desire to create and deliver becomes all-encompassing. Our mantra is to ignore the creative because that is, quite simply, the easy part. Understanding how to engage your audience and how to reach your goals is the hard part. Therefore, you need to define what success looks like which, as mentioned above, may not involve being able to forecast hard numbers until a way into the trial or implementation – although admittedly if you have undertaken a successful trial first, then you will be able to extrapolate those numbers onto other goals.

A point that can also not be overlooked is that you are going to need to identify a new breed of people who can develop capabilities as audience strategists. This is one of the earliest decisions you are going to have to make as you will need a small team who do not simply understand the customer from a marketing perspective, but also have the gumption to take an enterprise-wide view.

Engage Your Stakeholders

TIP 3

It is worth considering the breadth of people you are going to need to engage with internally. Our experience has shown that you can broadly speaking split these into three categories. First of all, there is the internal sponsor (i.e. budget holder) who, in an absolutely ideal world, would be you. Secondly, you need to engage the wider range of people responsible not just for the various audience engagement touch-points but also other aspects of the audience, such as insights and data. Our belief is that this is the first internal function you need to engage with, showing them what you are seeking to achieve before you start any of the work itself. We tend to do this through the persona mapping exercises as not only are you talking them through the approach but also involving them directly in its generation. Through these workshops you will garner valuable insights from their own experience and you will also be able to show how this approach differs from anything they are used to, whilst at the same time reassuring them that it is aligned to what they are already doing; remember, your watchword is 'alignment'. This is especially the case if there are other content strategies being developed in specific customer engagement silos.

Finally, there is senior management. This audience needs to understand the full scope of an audience engagement strategy in terms of how all channels are involved and aligned, and the fundamental shift it will create within the organisation with regards its approach to audience-centricity. Also, to be blunt, it is worth noting that you may or may not be able to do this with case study ROI to show them – remember, at the time of writing, the whole world of content marketing is in its first stage infancy and hard stats are few and far between.

Complete Audit

As you will read in the next two sections, conducting a content audit is an essential step in the creation of any content strategy. However, when considering the implementation steps for an audience engagement strategy you will need to go further than that in your analysis.

Understanding what other content marketing strategies are being implemented across your organisation is vital. Examples of silo content strategies could be marketing (of course) digital (if a separate function) CRM/contact centres, billing, and so on. It is important that in uncovering what other audience engagement functions within the company might be doing, you view these as strategies to be aligned with, not risks to your own implementation. If other functions have made the logical step to understand the power of content marketing and have put in place the processes to facilitate this then you will be able to incorporate this into your execution structure. Equally, if they have content vehicles already in place or being built that you can use then that is potentially a considerable saving.

Smart Investment

What the audit should have revealed is where the content vehicle gaps lie. For example, does a new microsite need to be built or can an existing one be expanded upon to fit your needs? Similarly, are there content creation or curation processes existing within your business that can be tapped into?

The two areas that will almost certainly require investment are people and technology. Section 4 expands upon what the actual requirement is; however, you will need content strategists to drive this forward and this should also include consideration of the use of external consultants with a track record of delivering such initiatives – bear in mind that it is highly unlikely that any agency you currently use will have the required breadth of skillset to help in any other capacity but the creation and delivery of content. You will also need to invest in software to automate the process as the alternative, as you will see, is to become mired in spreadsheet hell.

Be Flexible

There is a well-known phrase in military circles: 'no plan survives contact with the enemy' and we would suggest the same will apply when rolling out an audience engagement strategy. Clearly there is no 'enemy' per se, simply people internally who need to be brought on side. However, what you will see is that the indisputable logic of an audience engagement strategy approach means that other goals and audiences will be quickly identified that could be added.

Clearly you will have to pick your battles here as there has to be a sensible audience-led approach to the rollout. Simply randomly adding audiences, or overlaying new products/services onto existing engaged audiences without considering how this will impact the relationship, could be dangerous and negatively impact what work you have been doing.

Measure and Report

TIP 7

The entire ethos of an audience engagement strategy is built around governance and measurement. The planning phase defines the goals and the execution phases are designed around the ability to measure. Of course, this measurement will improve over time as the way in which your audiences engage with the content and your technical ability to track that improves. Again, expectation management will be required, especially as the reports may be quite basic to begin with, but they will become increasingly rich and powerful over time. And it should go without saying that clarity on how you will measure and report on any initial trial phase must be clearly identified at the very beginning.

Lights, Camera, Action

Within this section, we have hopefully set the scene for you in terms of making it clear what we mean by an audience engagement strategy as opposed to any other form of content marketing, and both where you are as an organisation in relation to this and where you should aim to be. We have also given you a rough sketch of what you are going to need to consider when approaching the development of your own audience engagement strategy. Now however, it is time get into the meat of the subject. The next section, therefore, will walk you through all of the essential elements of what an audience engagement strategy actually is. You will then be ready for section 4, which will tell you how to go about doing it.

SECTION

3

Understand

In this section we will walk you through all of the various aspects of an audience engagement strategy ensuring that we explain why you need to include all of these elements. We have written it in a sequential manner as if you were starting from scratch. Of course, the reality is that you will have a number of these components in place already. However, we would encourage you not to simply skim over a section because you recognise what we are talking about as in many cases you may find that we are extending what is already being done or looking at it in a different way. After all, one of the challenges in the marketing world is how we describe things as many of us tend to use the same description but mean very different things.

Bearing in mind that the entire essence of an audience engagement strategy is to build the strategy around the audience, there really is only one place to begin!

Begin by Understanding Your Audience

Understanding who your customers and prospects are and what they are interested in is the essential starting point for understanding your market. But as already alluded to in section 2, 'customers and prospects' are no longer a complete definition of everyone you should be communicating with. If we are all now publishers, a better definition is your 'audience'. In mapping out your strategy you need to start with all your stakeholders understanding the concept of your audience and who they are. To be clear, though, in performing the analysis: a customer has already bought something from you; a prospect is likely to buy something from you;

and then there is everyone else who may engage with you and be in your audience. Why would you be interested in people who are not customers or prospects? Let's start with who they are: the press, shareholders, government, stakeholders and the general public. All these parties can have a major impact on your reputation and, as we will discuss later, this is a key asset that you need to manage.

Managing your reputation is about managing your value as a business. By creating an overall and wider awareness, your brand becomes more accepted and recognised which makes the choice of purchasing your products or services easier. By developing a strategy that considers your wider audience you are taking care of your wider brand recognition. Plus, at a lower level these people may engage with you and become your advocates.

Good marketing in today's world is about being audience-centric, not brand or product-centric. It is only by adopting this approach that your company will be able to engage with your target audience and in so doing reap the associated business benefits. However, for the vast majority of brands this notion of audience-centricity, where it is the person, not the brand or products that are put at the heart of the communications strategy, is a challenging one. It is therefore important to understand what this means and how this will enable your company to engage with your target audience.

The key to success is your audience and so it is there that we must begin; and this, of course, throws up a mountain of challenges. For a start there will always be multiple audiences and purists will argue that every single individual person is a unique audience. They may be right in theory, but the practical delivery of

such a one-to-one marketing approach makes it largely untenable unless you happen to be a hyper-focused B2B brand. For any other company it is about bundling your audiences together into logical persona groups.

You will note that we have used the neutral term 'persona groups' not 'segments'. This isn't semantics, this is about breaking with some of the bad habits of most existing marketing strategies. Most traditional segmentation fits criteria that has only limited bearing on a content strategy. Rather than comparing and contrasting, let us outline what we are looking for when defining a persona grouping.

What are their interests? What do they care about or are kept awake thinking about? Who do they listen to, respect and turn to as influencers? You can probably see that questions such as these (and there are many more) are quite different to standard approaches to segmentation, although there are still some basic things we need to know such as what do they read, watch and consume? However, such insight is only the start of the audience insight process. It needs be layered on top with some attitudinal understanding that will allow us to, ultimately, understand their personas.

Thinking about your audience as personas is an essential element of good content marketing, mainly because it is critical to any form of writing. This manifests itself most obviously in journalism, particularly within the UK national press; a press understood the world over for the individualistic stances, politics and type of influence held by each publication. We have become used to the idea that the Telegraph is for right-wing conservatives, the Guardian for liberal lefties, the Mail for middle England women, and so on. However, as any journalist will tell you, the overwhelming thought one has when writing for such a publication is not 'What is our stance?' but 'What do the readers expect?' More importantly, when the news editor, section editors and their superiors are compiling each edition, they are selecting content that they know their readers will want to read. That is not just the mix of articles but the type of articles that suit the readers' personas. The result is a loyal readership which in many ways define themselves by the papers they read.

Of course, what is intriguing about marketing today is how people have changed so much in such a short period of time when it comes to the way they engage with content. Before the internet, the vast majority of content was simply consumed. In other words someone produced an advert, wrote an article or sent a piece of DM and the target audience chose whether to watch or read it. The company producing that content then hoped for a positive reaction and paid little attention to any reaction that was not positive.

By now you will see where we are going with this as that is simply not the case today. If you, as a company, produce an advert then your audience may talk about it with each other very publically online and it might not all be positive. However, more importantly their media world is now vastly more complex and becoming a part of it as a company wishing to grab their attention is increasingly difficult. If you think that they will sit there and passively absorb your brand or product message then you are wrong.

The fact is that there is simply too much compelling, gripping, interesting and absorbing content out there competing for your target audience's attention for you to stand a chance. You may want to continue broadcasting your message at them but the chances are that they are simply not paying any attention.

This is the point where most discussions about content marketing move on to the art of great storytelling. In principle we fully agree, one of the critical keys to success within content marketing is exactly that – great storytelling. Our concern is that too many brands are confusing this concept with 'telling their story' with the result that the only shift they have made is to move from saying 'buy our product' to now saying 'let me tell you about us'. It's still brand or product-centric, still self-obsessed and still broadcasting. The result? It's still not interesting to your target audience. Why should they care? After all, by taking such a stance you have shown that you are not interested in their stories, haven't you?

Instead, the better way to consider the change of stance required is to think first about the art of having a conversation. This is something all of us do very successfully every single day. Whether at home, at work, or down the proverbial pub, we all have conversations with other people. It does not matter what you are talking about, it is the fact that you are talking **with** someone. Not **at** someone.

A good conversation is reliant on one thing: having something to talk about that two or more people want to engage about. It does not matter whether it is the weather, politics, your next marketing campaign or what you are going to have for dinner tonight, a conversation is not a conversation without that fundamental point.

So if you, as a company, wish to engage **with** someone then you need to find that discussion topic that you both want to talk about. Of course, for most brands this does throw up a multitude of challenges. How will you identify the right topic? What have you,

as a company, the right to talk about that the audience will find interesting? The audience analysis will have identified the answers to these questions. Sometimes the answer is obvious and sometimes you might have to take one or two steps out of your obvious comfort zone to find the answer. For example, if you are a greetings cards company you may have to talk with your audience about making 'occasions' special.

We call this concept the 'point of mutuality' – finding the subject matter that both you and your audience can mutually engage about.

Mutuality says that you can find a subject matter that any audience would naturally associate with your brand and accept that you have the right to engage with them about. This may be because it is directly associated with what you sell – it is quite obvious that greetings cards are a part of celebrating an occasion such as a birthday, Christmas, Valentine's Day and so on. Therefore, talking as a brand about how to make occasions special is an unremarkable leap from your core business of selling cards. What it enables is for you to have an interaction with your target audience that you would not otherwise have achieved by simply telling them about your latest range of products.

However, the mutual subject matter could also be less about what you sell and more about what your audience is interested in – i.e. the essence of sponsorship. So if you as a brand already sponsor a sport, spending several thousand or even millions of pounds to do so, then your target audience will accept that you have the right to offer content around that sport, for example. And that content does not, of course, have to be simply the obvious as that content may already exist, leaving little room for you. So for example, if you sponsored the World Cup in Rio, perhaps you could offer travel advice, guidance on the stadiums, etc. Although if you are the one to serve up even the obvious content in the easiest, most accessible manner, then that could still be an attractive content marketing approach.

One word of warning, though, before we move on from the subject of sponsorship. Ensuring the point of mutuality for sponsorship should be equally as important. It is increasingly clear that brands that sponsor a sport, for example, and yet do not make or do anything vaguely relevant to sport are struggling to engage their audiences. If your goal is basic brand awareness, corporate hospitality or anything that does not involve connecting with consumers then sponsorship is fine. If not, then expect a hard time!

It is also worth touching upon the difference between B2C and B2B content marketing at this point. The simple answer is that there

is no difference in approach. The same audience insight needs to be undertaken, the same subject matter mutuality must be found. There are different challenges, of course, the most significant challenge being that you need to understand enough about your B2B audience to touch on a theme that they are going to care enough about to want to devote some of their precious business time to engage with you about. But this principle of 'what keeps them awake at night' has underpinned any worthwhile thought leadership campaign since time immemorial. In fact, a well-constructed B2B content marketing strategy allows for a far more impactful industry leadership position to be taken which many B2B brands would be wise to consider adopting.

Whatever the nature of your company, what is clear is that content marketing has redefined the meaning of 'understanding your audience'. We recognise this as a step-shift in thinking, the main ramifications of which are yet to be truly felt.

Analyse Customers, Prospects & Audience

The first job is to see what data you have got to perform this analysis. If you already have customers and a customer database this would be your start point. Depending on what data you have, you may find that there are 'clusters' of people around certain attributes. This is usually where you will define your segments. This is where we see a difference between segments and personas. Segmentation usually occurs around the attributes of customers that does not include what they are interested in or how they would like to see their content. For example, your postcode may be a factor that determines what segment you are in, but that will not tell me what your hobbies are. Therefore, let's look at an example of social demographic segmentation to see where this falls down if you want to have a conversation and engage with someone.

Take two men (no sneaking ahead to get the answer!); from a socio-demographic point of view these men are twins:

- Both male

- Both born 1948

- Both grew up in the UK

- Both have divorced and re-married

- Both have grown up children

- Both are very wealthy

- Both like to spend their holidays in the Alps

- Both are world famous

If you follow a segmentation method that only looks at these attributes, these two men would get the same messages (in the same style), from you.

They are in fact Ozzy Osbourne & Prince Charles. There is probably little chance that they would both respond to the same message or the same content! This is an extreme example to make the point, but even for the rest of us segmentation does not work for engaging communications. However, it does have a place in our planning and strategy efforts. Our market strategy requires

that we at least know how many people we want to address, how many we would like to become customers and what share of the market that we have. Why we need to know this is a function of budgets. We will have a finite amount of money in order to reach this audience, so we need to know who (and how many) we are aiming to engage.

You may have an existing segmentation strategy. When embarking on an intelligent engagement strategy through content you need to align to this and not disregard it. Your content personas will 'borrow' from the existing insight that you have with your segments. It will, of course, be very dependent on how much information and how your segments have been created as to how much alignment you will get – one example we have seen was actually just the channels that some customers used to access the client's services, it did not tell us anything about the individuals that might be in that group. The best segmentation strategies that align to what you will need for identifying personas are 'needs' based segmentation. These are usually more lifestyle based and try to identify why your customer needs your product. Whilst imperfect as discussed above it does provide a better start point.

Personas

Typically, you should have no more than seven personas. This is simply because it is not possible to differentiate one piece of content more than seven different ways. What this means is that it is not simply the topics of mutuality that define the personas, it is also how the story is told. You will have the same basic ideas told in different ways for different personas. Consider what and how you tell Mum about a venue (Where is the café? Where is the childcare?) versus how you tell the child (What games can I play? What is fun to do here?). It is the same basic information, but it focuses on different areas and is told in different ways – although

remember, some of your content is about your products and services, it is not all about the mutual topics. As another example, a website supporting a technical device may have advanced users and beginners. Each will have different needs from the content but it is based upon the same information.

What the personas allow you to do, as described above, is write (or create) for someone specifically. For example, we know of a company with a technical product set and the engineers wrote the user manuals. The problem is that without personas to guide them, they ended up writing for themselves.

Discovering Mutuality

If you have already been publishing something digitally, be it a monthly magazine, a newsletter or a blog, you have the potential to track what people have been reading. In order to 'listen', sometimes we have to start the conversation to get it going. What you may not have done in this publishing effort is to listen closely to which topics in your outpourings have had the best engagement. This is where technology can now help. By 'tagging' your content you can start to understand what audience members are interested in what topics. These topic clusters will start to form your mutuality stories.

If you have already got a user group or forum where customers can exchange comments and ideas, just listening to this can give you the areas of interest. For example Coca-Cola found that a common question on their forum was a recipe for a Coca-Cola cake. This led to the development of an area devoted to food and recipes. Whilst 'food' might have seemed obvious given their product, it was not an area of focus or topic of mutuality before they 'listened'.

This diagram shows you the core elements that we need to start to define our engagement strategy. It is worth viewing the next items (covered off in the next two chapters) that you will need to develop in order to see what you need to think about in defining your personas. The process is iterative around these elements because as you develop each part it will give you ideas about how you need to adjust other parts. As you start publishing on subjects wider than your own products and services you will learn a lot more that will improve your insight on your audience and change your strategy.

Journeys

For an audience engagement strategy to work for your company, you must have a clear understanding of what your goal actually is. This is as equally key an element to either understanding your audience as already discussed or, as we shall come onto later, defining your content pillars.

Defining your audience engagement strategy goal is what we refer to as your 'engagement cycle mapping'; in other words, it is a mapping of the audience journey. This is about how you align the target objective of your audience – i.e. to satisfy a need or desire – with your own commercial objective – i.e. to sell your product or service to that target audience. What should, therefore, be clear is that this is not the same as your sales cycle. The audience engagement cycle map is about the audience's journey. Such journeys are not linear and **are** very personal. In other words, an audience's journey is highly unlikely to follow the nice straight lines of your sales cycle and instead each persona will take

a different route and undergo different decision-making processes. The resulting audience engagement cycle map, which is the cumulative output of the ongoing process of understanding your audience, defining your goals and building your content pillars, takes this into account. The maps are about creating a matrix of the storylines, pillars and personas so that an individual target audience could start anywhere within the process and end up engaged with you, potentially buying your product or service if that is your desired business outcome.

So the goal is about what you want and then understanding how to take your audience on a journey that will get them there. It is, in short, about defining the audience journey that the individual will take.

There are many aspects to the personas that you need to discover; however, these can be broken down into four levels of understanding. Together, these insights will allow you to build and continually evolve an audience engagement strategy that takes the various target audience personas on the desired journey.

1. Perceptions & Attitude

First of all, it is about understanding perceptions and attitudes. This was highlighted in the previous chapter. The audience journey determines the subjective hurdles that the content strategy must overcome. For example, you might love the Virgin brand but prefer to fly with British Airways. This is an attitudinal position that forms part of your persona. A Virgin Atlantic audience engagement strategy must therefore seek to overcome your utterly subjective attachment to British Airways whilst conversely the British Airways strategy needs to build upon that subjectivity to reinforce it. That means that for British Airways to simply seek to engage you about the brand loyalty you already have will not take you any further on your own personal audience journey with British Airways.

Perhaps this is because the challenge both brands face is that while you like flying, you actually prefer to holiday in the UK. What this means is that both British Airways and Virgin Atlantic have a battle to engage with people like you about holidaying by flying abroad. That is the audience journey that needs to be mapped, with the brand perception woven into that process.

The Intelligent Marketing Institute

2. Trigger Points

This weaves into the second point, understanding the trigger points to purchase. In other words, when do you need to be influencing the target audience on their decision-making journey? Indeed, how much do you need to be the trigger for the decision to consider purchasing in the first place? For example, how much should British Airways and Virgin Atlantic convince you to fly for leisure and therefore prompt you into entering their purchasing funnel in the first place? As such, how much effort needs to be put into feeding the target audience into the funnel rather than simply converting those already within it? Are you better fighting to grow your existing market share within today's market, or growing the market? And then you need to understand how your existing sales cycle needs to support the audience-centric view that pulls people into the funnel in the first place – e.g. the ease of booking a flight as a family; information on where best to holiday as a family; links to family-friendly hotels and resorts; etc.

3. Channels

The third point is regards the channels themselves. When mapping the audience journey, you need to understand what the audience journey will be from a media perspective. This is 'media' in the broadest sense and assumes an integrated strategy that seamlessly underpins any above the line or below the line activities with the same content strategy. So the target audience would be engaged with the same generic content approach regardless as to whether they received a piece of direct mail, were sent a viral video link by a friend or read the opinion of a journalist in a newspaper.

3. Channels Continued

The key to the integrated channel strategy is to ensure that it is targeted appropriately so that the right sort of content is reaching the various personas through the correct forms of media. In a purely speculative sense (using the above three channel examples only), it would look like Virgin Atlantic or British Airways: a) posting a brochure with great family holiday destinations for young families as reviewed by young families; b) creating an amusing viral video of car family trauma (think National Lampoon's *European Vacation* brought up to date); and c) pitching a national newspaper with the idea of sending two journalists on the two different types of holiday to compare and contrast the happiness factor (in UK Government style!). All three of these approaches via the three different channels, as well as many others that could be listed, would enter the target audience's media world and have a high percentage chance of being seen. The audience journey would then be crafted to take the audience onto the next logical step in the journey. For simplicity's sake, let's assume that's a microsite. This specifically crafted journey would take the audience to the next logical engagement point. That may or may not be where they are then sold to, depending on whether that is the next logical step in the journey. Perhaps, as would arguably be the case in this example, it is a content site that creates and curates ideas about family holidays for under 10s and becomes a must-see resource for myself and my wife when thinking about our next family holiday. Regardless of whether that led to a sale for either airline or not, the fact that they have the audience captured, the future opportunity to sell, the greater brand empathy as well as the information they can ascertain from my content viewing on that microsite, would be worth the investment alone.

A key point to note, as you can see from this example, is that it is not just about a great TV advert idea or other 'Big Idea'. Instead, it is about 'Long Ideas' that any advert has to carry through with the next steps of the journey. This is the part most brands are yet to achieve and is what the audience engagement strategy is about helping you do.

4. Influencers

The fourth and final point is about influencers. It was once said that the definition of PR is that you buy something because you heard you ought to. Whether you agree or not, it is certainly the case that many people have not bought something because they have been warned not to! As such, influencers matter. Therefore, be it trusted third parties, such as journalists and bloggers, through to the wide circle of influencers that permeate the average person's social media world, any company that is seeking to plan an audience journey must build influencer relations into that plan.

Think Sustain, Not Just Campaign

At this point an essential point must be made with regards the concept of 'audience journeys'. A journey suggests a fixed destination and that could easily be assumed to be the sale. Whilst it is entirely probable that the audience journey would lead directly to a sale, it would be wrong to think in such linear terms. Why, for example, should it simply be thought of as **a** sale? Why not repeat sales? However, more importantly, that sale may never come directly but through other ways. They could become an influencer who never buys but tells others of the offer, or does not buy that family holiday (as in the example above) but instead opts to fly through that airline for business. The point to note is that if the primary goal is to attract customers, then this could happen immediately or at any time in the future and when it does happen the audience engagement strategy will play an essential role in sustaining their interest and loyalty in your company.

What is important here is that the outcome may not be a singular outcome. Crucially, it will almost certainly be felt over a period of time, perhaps for the entire lifetime of that target audience. The power of a successful audience engagement strategy is that such a prolonged outcome is entirely expected.

Content marketing lends itself to sustained audience engagement. That does not mean that campaigning is dead, it just means that campaigning is a stepping stone in the audience journey and must be interlinked with the wider strategy to create the desired outcome. For example, above we mentioned the increasingly common tactic of driving the audience directly to a microsite and ensuring that every aspect of the marketing communications activities is built around that initial objective.

This is why we think of the audience journey as an engagement cycle. It will continually evolve as the relationship between the brand and the individual evolves, as their interests change and the way they wish to engage or are influenced adapts over time. The process of defining the personas, audience journeys and content pillars will be ongoing – it is never singularly defined at one point in time. The result will be a matrix of adapting storylines, pillars and personas so that a person could start anywhere on the journey and end up engaged with you (potentially, buying your product(s) or service(s) if that is your goal).

As such, there is no end point. There are goals, but these are continually adapted as the target audience travels on their own personal journey with your brand. The magic ingredients to making this a success then lie within the content pillars and editorial storylines.

Content Pillars & Editorial Calendar

The one area we have observed where most brands are failing at content marketing programmes is the planning of the content itself. Identifying, planning, scheduling and then delivering the right content on an ongoing basis that will sustain the target audience's interest is a considerable step change from the existing marketing communications campaigns of the vast majority of companies today. It is for this reason that we think of the development of the content pillars and the subsequent editorial calendar as being the magic ingredients that will make your content strategy fly.

The content pillars sit alongside the audience insight process and audience engagement cycle mapping as the ongoing content strategy alignment for your organisation. Both of these processes have been outlined previously: the audience insight process identifies the target audience personas and the point of subject area mutuality between your brand and the target audience; the audience engagement cycle maps are formed when you define your content marketing goals and develop the resulting audience journeys.

What the content pillars then do is to align the content to the audience personas and your business objectives. They are the glue that binds the whole programme together.

From the content pillars will come the editorial calendar which is the live planning layer of the entire content marketing programme. The content pillars identify the core content themes and storylines that will enable your company to produce the right sort of content that the audience will engage with. It then determines which channels and platforms will be used within the audience engagement programme itself.

Defining the Content Pillars

Content pillars are the core themes that stretch from the point of mutuality. So for example, if you are a bank selling mortgages then the point of mutuality could be property. The content pillars might then be determined as 'house selling & buying', 'renovations & improvements', 'extensions', and 'tradesmen & builders'. How these will have been determined will, of course, have been based upon the insight into your audience personas, so those four examples have been listed simply as generic examples.

These content pillars sit on top of a foundation layer of attributes that will govern the type of content pillars that are appropriate for your company. Typically these fall into the four storytelling elements of 'Entertain', 'Educate', 'Convince' and 'Inspire'. In other words, a successful content pillar theme would contain one or more of these elements.

At the same time it could be that the point of mutuality is defined more by the audience persona than anything your company actually offers as a product or service. This may already have led your brand to engage in, for example, sports sponsorship. In that case, the content pillars would be built around that point of mutuality, for example your brand's existing Formula One car sponsorship.

When deciding the content pillars, the following three characteristics must be used as the litmus test as to whether the topic is viable for your brand and your audience:

1. Editorial Interest

This may seem incredibly obvious, but ultimately it has to be a topic that can be editorialised and therefore have editorial interest. In other words, is it a broad enough and engaging enough a topic that a sequence of editorial content, potentially one that is perpetually evolving, can be created? It is a fact that some topics are simply far too narrow for this to be possible in a way that the publisher (your brand) and the reader (your target audience) can sustain.

This is not only an exceptionally important point when it comes to the viability of a content pillar subject from an editorial interest point of view, but also from a content production perspective. Broadly speaking, you will have three potential sources of content: content you create yourselves using your own writers; content you curate from other sources such as the web; and content you co-create with your audience. If the topic is viable you will be able to create, curate and co-create it indefinitely.

2. Actionable

Sadly, the maxim of 'create it and they will come' does not apply to any form of published content. That means that you are going to have to attract your target audience to your content. To do so will require marketing communications campaigns and ongoing programmes that reach your audience and draw them in to become regular consumers of your content. So any content pillar subject must be interesting and compelling enough that activities can be created that will do that. Admittedly, it is possible that even the driest subject matter could have creative treatment that achieves this goal. However, the ability to create a one-off brilliant campaign does not satisfy the litmus test as that campaign will simply have to be followed up with a sequence of other campaigns to continue to reach and drive audiences.

3. Sustainable

The requirement for the subject to be sustained over time has already been referred to in the above, but it is important enough to require specific highlighting. Whilst accepting that it is possible for a content pillar to have a short shelf-life, this will be the exception not the norm. So each and every content pillar has to be a subject matter that can be sustained, otherwise you will invest effort reaching and creating an audience that you will ultimately risk losing.

Controlling the Content

Once the content pillars have been initially defined – and bearing in mind that this could be altered over time as you continually analyse your content strategy alignment – you will be able to start the ball rolling on your editorial calendar.

As the planning tool and process that will govern the day-to-day operation of your audience engagement strategy, the editorial calendar will become a standard part of your marketing planning. Do not think of your editorial calendar as simply being a list of upcoming content that needs to be created, curated or co-created. Instead, think of it as being the living essence of your audience engagement strategy. Put simply, a well-designed and executed editorial calendar will allow you to plan, target, reach and influence your target audiences to meet your business goals – more on how this works will be explained in section 4. Having said that, it does also fulfil the core publishing function of defining what content needs to be produced at any given time.

Therefore, the editorial calendar acts as the planning tool for the content that needs delivering to the target audience. This will broadly come in three potential forms. Firstly 'news', which is a catch-all term for anything that is new and relevant and also includes your company's ability to 'newsjack' a topical story of the day. Secondly 'features', which is non-time-specific content that in a B2B context is often referred to simply as thought leadership. Finally there is 'campaigning', which borrows a journalistic term to govern the targeted reference around a given story or topic. This might be to support a marketing communications campaign activity that is drawing the audience in, or a genuine point that you, as a business, wish to promote to your target audience.

The editorial calendar will also define the way in which any individual piece of content will be used and this in turn will define how it is drafted. This is fairly straightforward and should come naturally – i.e. the way you draft a piece of content for social media is different for a website/microsite, the way it is drafted for an ad is different to the way it would be drafted long-form for a newsletter and so on. However, where you as a brand publisher must ensure that you take the widest possible view of content is in deciding the multimedia format.

Thanks to the rise of the internet, text-based content has enjoyed a dominant resurgence over the audio and visual upstarts of the 20th century. However, this is in the process of changing once again. Video, especially, is reasserting itself as a powerful content format made possible by the technological improvements to internet and mobile phone bandwidth of the past few years. More on this in chapter 8 in this section.

Of course, the format of the content will also dovetail into the way in which the content is delivered. By having this plotted within the editorial calendar, this integrated execution becomes more efficient and the content strategy programme more effective. Your team, including any third party agencies, will be able to clearly see what content is being produced and their role in activating it. In addition to any actions that need to be taken around the content, the editorial calendar can also define how engagement, interaction and next step triggers can be built around the content to ensure maximum audience participation.

The editorial calendar is a crucial part of delivering the audience journeys that were mapped within the audience engagement cycle maps. The editorial calendar is a strategic tool, not simply a content list. As such, it must be constructed in a way that enables your organisation to deliver the audience journeys. In other words, the audience engagement cycle maps will have defined what the audience journeys are for each persona. So, the editorial calendar will ensure the provision of the content that is required to deliver these journeys.

Hopefully it is now clear how important the editorial calendar is. What should also be clear is that as a brand publisher, regular editorial planning meetings will become a core aspect of your marketing communications routine with the editorial calendar acting as the central dashboard for that process.

Reputation Management

It remains a shocking fact that the majority of businesses today still do not have a crisis communications plan in place. Despite the fact that today's media is buoyed by a near perpetual cycle of business crises, too few businesses are prepared to pay any attention to the commercial value of their reputation. It is perhaps, therefore, ironic that many companies remain fearful of engaging with their target audiences, especially online, for fear of the negative impact it might have upon their reputation. This is a knee-jerk instinctive reaction to a wider problem they are simply not prepared to face up to. However, it does mean that any shift to a content-led approach may be stillborn due to nothing more than a gut reaction from an alarmist management team.

Of course, this fear is stoked by the embarrassingly large number of instances when companies have got their online communications hideously wrong. Every year social media commentators revel in trawling over the worst examples of social media campaigns that have backfired, negative campaigns led by upset customers that have gone viral and damaged a brand, and so on. As such, any serious consideration of a content marketing strategy must build reputation management into its development from the very start.

Why Reputation Management is Essential Within Any Content Marketing

Putting the numerous examples of reputation disasters to one side for a moment, it is important to understand why reputation management matters so much when it comes to content marketing in whatever degree of maturity you like.

First of all the most obvious point which, sadly, most brands refuse to accept; if you do not manage your reputation then the public and your customers will. In other words, if you do not face up to and address issues around your brand's reputation then others will do so for you with potentially disastrous consequences. This ownership of your brand reputation may be highly public, through social media, or simply spread through word of mouth and dinner party sentiment. Whatever the channel, the result is the same; other people have more control over your brand's reputation than you do.

Why this matters for content marketing is because, as we have already stressed, by embarking upon a content-led approach you are by definition improving your audience engagement. However, by engaging with your audience you are exposing your brand to whatever that audience may already think and feel about your company. Content cannot exist in a reputation vacuum. In other words

those thoughts and feelings will seep through with the potential to overshadow your entire audience engagement programme.

This is largely because of the second point, the impact of the digital and social media engagement channel. Whilst the rise of online engagement has been the catalyst behind the current rise of content marketing, it has also had deeply impactful consequences on reputation management. The advent of social media platforms such as Twitter and Facebook, as well as blogs and other mediums for citizen journalism, has meant that it has never been easier for anyone to voice their opinion about your brand, and then to be heard and be repeated. Try to engage with this audience without proper reputation management planning, regardless as to whether it is part of a deliberate content marketing strategy, and you could fan the flames of any negative sentimentality very easily and very quickly. Of course, be careful who you let read that last sentence as taken out of context it can play to knee-jerk instincts to not engage.

The third point is regards another knee-jerk reaction that has been seen within management teams, namely the fear about having an opinion. What if someone disagrees? What if we are wrong? What if it gives something away to the competition? All are valid questions around which your editorial calendar needs to be carefully planned. However, the spirit of engagement is to have an opinion. If you do not have an opinion then anything you are saying becomes increasingly uninteresting and that will thoroughly undermine your content strategy.

There are dangers of scoring an own goal with your own content, which is the fourth point that needs making. Ask yourself this question, how possible is it that you and your marketing communications teams do not know everything that is going on within your organisation? You are in a rarefied position if the answer is not simply 'very possible', probably for very innocent reasons around a lack of internal communication by your management colleagues. The challenge therefore exists around ensuring that anything you put out as content does not in some way conflict with anything else your business might be up to – an easy example would be about talking about how to save money and then finding out that your business is about to raise its prices. The key, obviously, is integration and alignment around the editorial calendar.

The final point worth making about the importance of reputation management within content marketing is about detractors. As the saying goes, you cannot please all of the people all of the time. Given the potential loudhailer that social media gives anyone with a negative view towards your brand then it is no wonder that any company is at risk from having highly vocal detractors – of course, just because they are vocal does not mean anyone is necessarily listening. However, that is why detractor engagement is an important part of reputation management planning.

Reputation Management and Content Marketing – a Match Made in Heaven

There is a saying amongst reputation management professionals: 'never let an issue become a crisis'. And yet it is clear that the vast majority of brands continue to do exactly that due to ignorance and a lack of preparedness. That is why when you step back and consider the ramifications of the five points made above, it is clear why so many companies are making so many reputation errors.

The good news is that a mature audience engagement strategy will, by default, address this lack of reputation management planning. This is because at the heart of a content-led approach **is** planning.

Consider the key features of the audience engagement strategy as we have described it in the previous three chapters: you must understand your audience; you must plan the audience journeys; and you must define the content pillars which then become the foundation of your ongoing editorial calendar. These are all the raw insights that are needed within your reputation planning. And all of this insight is perpetually renewed.

The only thing that is required is to interpret these insights from a reputation management perspective. In other words, whilst planning for the positive impact that the audience engagement strategy will have in terms of meeting your business objectives, consider the potential negative complications at the same time.

Building Reputation Management Into Content Planning

To make it simple, we have boiled how to build reputation management into content strategy planning down to four processes:

1. Reputation Risk Audit Around Content Themes

Reputation risk audits are a proven part of crisis communications planning. In that context it involves the analysis of the business to identify the risks to the company's reputation, looking at the propensity for the risk to occur and the damage to the business should it occur. This allows the crisis plan to be developed in an appropriate manner that is relative to each risk.

The same approach to cross-business analysis is done within a content marketing perspective. However, the difference is that one is analysing that risk purely from the perspective of the content pillars. Additionally, the focus is on avoiding creating reputation risk issues rather than managing issues that could potentially already exist. As such, the aim is to clearly identify reputation risk issues that could occur within a content pillar, ensure these are flagged and highlighted to the marketing communications teams and then ensure that they are avoided. Worth mentioning, of course, that this is not a one-off exercise and has to be done in conjunction with point two below.

2. Align the Editorial Calendar With Business Activity

It is essential that a process is put in place which ensures that the editorial calendar is aligned with events within the business.

How this is achieved will vary from business to business as ideally it would dovetail into existing internal lines of communication. However, the net result has to be that nothing should be published that runs the risk of creating a reputation own goal. Indeed, focusing on the development of this process will be invaluable for any marketing communications team as it will not only avoid embarrassing reputation mistakes that could have been easily avoided in the planning process but also help in a crisis.

3. Real-Time Event Monitoring

Just as important as the internal process above is an outward-facing analysis of real world events. This is more likely to be a process that your social media team already has in place than any of the others within this list. The reason is partly because commenting on real world events has often been seen as easy fodder for a brand's social media team. However, dreadful examples exist of where brands have got this wrong and in turn faced considerable public backlash for trying to involve their brand in a wholly inappropriate manner. This has made most social media teams incredibly wary of using real-world events as hooks unless there is an obvious and, often, direct link.

From a wider reputation management perspective, it is worth taking this one step further and ensuring that the content team is actively considering how any content that is about to be published could be construed in relation to real world events. From a planning perspective, there is considerable merit in assessing what sort of real world events should be particularly monitored for and alerts put in place to ensure checks are made before the content is activated. This would form part of the approvals process that is point four below.

4. Approvals Process

When it comes to reputation management, the approvals process is the single most important step. Approving content is not just about checking spelling and grammar, house style, brand values and so on. From a reputation management perspective it is about being the final gatekeeper to ensure that the above three processes have been carried out correctly.

As such, our recommended approach to the approvals process is to mimic the tried and tested approach taken within the newspaper industry. There, drafted content is typically assessed at least twice; first by the news editor, then the sub-editor. Although in reality several deputies will also have run their eye over the copy and usually the editor as well. The result is that not only is the resulting article newsworthy and relevant for the readership but it is also risk assessed. Setting up a system that imitates this risk analysis will be vital for your content strategy delivery. However, it should be speedy; you cannot wait for two weeks for approval on every piece of content. For this reason we also suggest that you need the editorial organisation structures that go with this process

Given that your audience engagement will not be starting from scratch, you may already find yourself dealing with detractors and therefore have concerns about how a content marketing strategy will work in such an environment. From that perspective, if you don't have one already, then a well thought through detractor engagement plan must sit within your reputation management planning. A detractor engagement plan builds a response strategy to real and potential detractor comments in terms of how and when to respond, tone of voice and guidelines on the type of content that should be used within a response. As such, it forms the next step within your real-time social media monitoring while at the same time enabling the organisation to offer a single, consistent response to detractors regardless of whether online, in-store, through the contact centre and so on.

On the subject of detractors, it also worth noting that if your company faces a significant problem with sustained criticism of the brand, products and/or services, then a content strategy is one viable and proven method of dealing with the problem.

In other words, your business goal will be to reduce the impact of such detractors and that can be done by developing a content strategy that promotes positive sentiment. Diluting negative sentiment and developing advocates is the single most effective means of dealing with such issues.

At the same time, if your brand has suffered significant reputation damage from a crisis, then a content strategy can be similarly powerful in rebuilding your brand reputation.

Be in Control

The overwhelming message should therefore be clear that rather than creating reputation management concerns, content marketing will be an enabler of greater reputation management **control** within your organisation. By embedding the processes outlined above within your marketing communications and customer engagement processes, you will be weaving reputation management into your day-to-day engagement strategy. Few companies have that to date. Therefore, given the board level focus that increasingly surrounds reputation management, its ability to play such a positive role in enforcing best practice is a significant positive business outcome of a content marketing approach.

In this chapter

- Engaging Audiences
- Digital Journeys

From Engagement to Participation

If you are going to take your target audience on a pre-determined journey, as identified within your audience engagement strategy, then you are by necessity committing yourself to a prolonged engagement with that target audience. Few brands are prepared for the ramifications of engaging with an audience over a sustained period of time and from a marketing perspective it throws up an array of new challenges.

The first challenge is that you are going to have to pay as much attention to sustaining the audience's interest as attracting it in the first place. This will necessitate a more considered approach to the activities you undertake within your own digital environments – be it a social media platform like Facebook, Twitter or LinkedIn, and most importantly within your own web domains.

The closest most companies have got to sustained engagement with a target audience is through running a Facebook page or Twitter feed and the creation and maintenance of a blog. Whereas many companies continue to enjoy acceptable results from running a Facebook page, in recent times blogs have increasingly fallen out of fashion with the predominant reason given that they are hard to maintain. This is no doubt the case if you do not have a content strategy. However, the truth as to why many blogs are abandoned or stagnate is that they fail to stimulate a response. Bearing in mind that a blog is nothing more than a web name for short pieces of content, it is important to understand why they are deemed to be failing.

The Trial of the Blog

Why do blogs not receive comments? It is a question that bamboozles many companies as comments are often taken as a measure of how interested and engaged the audience is. However, the better question to be asking would be how do I run a blog that generates and tracks engagement? The answer lies in the style and structure of the blog.

A blog is not a chore. It is not something that must be fed every week with 150 plus words as a 'to do' list action. A blog is a content platform and any good content platform that wants to attract and sustain an audience must contain some vital ingredients.

First of all, it must be treated as an editorial platform within your content strategy. As such, it must be governed by an editorial calendar and set up to meet the editorial needs of one or more of your target audience personas. Therefore, it has to be focused around the point of mutuality that you have identified and act as a delivery channel for your content pillars.

What that then looks like is a blog that is not a simple self-serving vehicle for your brand, product or service – far too many blogs are built around the single issue that the company would like the audience to read about. This is 'broadcasting' at its worst with little to no consideration about what will make an interesting and engaging read for the target audience. Indeed, the target audience's own needs and interests are largely ignored. No wonder, therefore, that the audience loses interest and certainly rarely comments. After all, for someone to comment suggests that they feel engaged. Going back then to the principle of content marketing best practice about finding the point of mutuality, a blogger should not expect a comment to be submitted if the reader is not engaged. To achieve that, the topic must be of mutual interest and not just a self-serving diatribe by the writer on behalf of the company.

Equally important is the ability for the blog to be found. There is no place for a 'build it and they will come' mentality in content marketing. The blog content needs to be promoted and, crucially, form part of the overall audience engagement strategy that is being implemented over multiple channels. The blog, therefore, becomes another expression of that content which has the critical ability to sustain the engagement and interest of the target audience.

On that point, many blogs are not very user-friendly. It is hard to search around topics, hard to navigate and ends up becoming a stream of disconnected articles. The importance of user experience online is well known and from a content point of view is often woefully overlooked.

The Content Mix

A blog is one expression of your content on your own site. In fact, calling it a blog is probably a misnomer due to many of the negative connotations attached to the activity. A better way to think of it would be as the editorial, regardless of whether the format is text, image or video based.

As an activity it will almost certainly reside alongside a range of other engagement activities on your website if you are going to sustain the audience's interest. And, of course, the advantage of running such sustained audience engagement on your own website (be it your corporate site or one set up separately as an engagement vehicle) is that you are not at the mercy of a social media platform subjecting you to changes beyond your control with the resulting expense of reacting to that change. Nor do you face the uncertainties about whether they are your audience or, as many argue, Facebook's. If they are on your own website such uncertainties do not exist with the significant added benefit that you have the opportunity to track what your audience reads and consumes.

Of course, just because the audience has been attracted to your website does not mean that they should be treated as a single collective. The principle of specific journey maps for your various target audience personas still applies. As such the range of content and engagement activities will be comprehensive enough to encompass all of these persona types. Therefore, in the same way that the content you are producing will be designed to reflect the needs of the personas, so will the engagement activities. What those engagement activities consist of will be determined by experience of what works for that persona type and the creativity of your team.

For example, a leading UK recruiter of engineers, that had identified as the point of mutuality the need to represent the overlooked voice of UK engineers, built a microsite containing among other engagement activities an interactive survey. This allowed engineers to understand the results from an industry, sector, peer and personal perspective and to share those results accordingly.

Engagement to Participation

Any content and accompanying engagement activities are essential for sustaining the audience interest. However, to truly engage your audience, the goal should be audience participation. In other words, to strive beyond sustained engagement to achieve proactive involvement by the target audience through submitted content and visible interaction.

Social media platforms, naturally, have such visible interaction at their heart. A Facebook 'like' or a submitted post are visible signs that your audience has engaged with your content and you need to replicate this on your own website. Although do bear in mind that your goal must remain the sustained engagement of your audience and therefore measuring the quantity of 'likes' for example is a false statistic unless you can track the continued 'likes' of an individual. If you do not do that then what you are actually capturing is that at some point someone 'liked' your content and you lack the evidence as to whether that individual has sustained their interest – this is a major point of criticism of existing social media platforms for brand to audience engagement.

If you are able to achieve participation then you can deem your audience to be truly engaged. It is the most visible way to demonstrate that the point of mutuality you identified and the resulting content pillars are perfectly suited for the personas of your target audience and that your brand is having a mature content conversation with your target audience. It also has the benefits of having user generated content supplementing the content you are already creating and/or curating as well as providing a higher degree of authenticity around your audience engagement which will, in turn, stimulate new audiences to greater levels of sustained engagement. Ultimately,

participation creates a patina of brand independence for your content strategy and audiences will respond better within such an environment.

Tying it All Together

Clearly striving for participation is moot if you fail to attract the audience in the first place. The planning of digital journeys, as already outlined in this book, empowers you with the ability to tie all your marketing and communications activities together to deliver the target audience to your chosen web environment. As a simple example, the campaign that was wrapped around the interactive survey of engineers referenced above used a mixture of marketing (e-mails to engineer candidates on their database) and PR activities (editorial secured in national newspapers and trade magazines) to attract engineers to the site.

Of course, it is when considering the digital journey that many brands are quite rightly attracted to using existing social media platforms rather than making the investment required to create their own engaging website environment. The single advantage that Facebook, Twitter and so on have is that they have an enormous existing audience already there with the associated social sharing capabilities to spread your message. However, using a social media platform and having your own website for the audience engagement are not mutually exclusive and should work in tandem

On the point of mutual exclusivity, digital and physical should also be seen as two sides of the same coin. Just because digital is the natural environment for a sustained engagement does not mean that the engagement should only ever reside digitally. For example, physical events as a means of engagement and, indeed, participation are a powerful tool for sustaining interest. In fact, if you are a high street retailer it may also be a desired business outcome of the audience engagement strategy by driving footfall in store.

However, what cannot be ignored is that journey planning and creativity must work in concert. Where journey planning will ensure better business outcomes, so the creativity will ensure a better audience experience. One without the other is a recipe for failure.

The Art of Storytelling

It was a dark and stormy night; the rain fell in torrents. And so continues the most stereotypical opening to any book you could possibly imagine. Indeed, virtually any story could begin with those words from a bestselling work of fiction worthy of the Booker prize through to the latest children's novel. Although let us have some pity for poor Edward Bulwer-Lytton to whose 1830 novel, *Paul Clifford*, the sentence belongs. Bulwer-Lytton's opening words to that novel may be frequently parodied but he was a man of significant writing prowess; he did, after all, coin other great phrases including 'the pen is mightier than the sword'.

The point, however, is that those few words capture many of the facets of storytelling. It grabs the reader's attention, it makes you want to read on, it puts you in a setting you can easily identify with. All of that in just twelve words and fifty-eight characters (with spaces).

As a company wanting to engage your audience, you have no choice but to consider the art of storytelling. To fail to do so is to remain stuck in the 'broadcasting' rut of shouting your messages at your target audience in the vain hope that anyone can be bothered to listen; something fewer and fewer people are prepared to do in today's hyper-media world.

You also have to appreciate that your audience is increasingly sophisticated when it comes to the role of being the audience, which if you pause and reflect for a moment you will realise is the quid pro quo to the art of storytelling. Sit back and look at the world around you for a moment and you will appreciate how sophisticated the modern audience has become. The trilogy has given way to the seven volume epic as a matter of course; TV series routinely contain meta-plots that span several seasons of episodes; and Christmas adverts occasionally do nothing other than tell a simple story for three minutes. We accept all of this as normal and it is because your audience has become very sophisticated at being an audience.

As a brand publisher you are going to have to take this into consideration. However, the art of storytelling for a brand is far more wide-ranging than popular entertainment. It must also span the art of journalistic storytelling as well as taking into account that there is a purpose behind the story, in the same way that a political party must always find a compelling narrative to convey their vision of how the voter will benefit by voting in their favour.

Lessons From Fleet Street

It should hopefully come as no surprise that there is a specific art to journalistic storytelling, in particular, how journalists grab and retain a reader's interest both throughout the newspaper and within any individual article.

Starting with the articles themselves, it is no simple challenge to attract a reader to read any individual article, and even harder still to retain their interest to read the entire piece. In fact, retaining the reader's interest is not necessarily the primary objective of the writer. Instead, the journalist must provide the information within the news article in a way that satisfies the reader's requirements.

To put that into perspective, you need to understand the components of a news article and how this leads to its typical structure. This, of course, starts with the headline which, it should be noted, is not written by the reporter. That is because the headline is meant to grab the reader's eye and is not designed to tell the story. It is, if you like, the advert for the article and is therefore written by the sub-editor. In reality, the journalist's storytelling work begins with the intro; that single sentence that has more work to do than could possibly be imagined. A standard intro for an average news story must:

- Convey the key elements of the story in a single sentence so that the reader can read that sentence alone and still be satisfactorily informed about that news item;

- Make the story appear interesting enough to entice the reader to read on, while at the same time;

- Allow the reader to self-select whether it is the type of story they wish to devote time to reading.

All of that in a single sentence. To put the above into context, if the news article is about the government making changes to the way pre-school childcare is funded then a non-parent will want to understand the key facts from the intro but is unlikely to want to read more. However, a parent will want to understand the key facts and decide whether they have time and/or desire to read on. If the intro to the story is strong enough, that parent is going to make the time and continue reading.

The journalist then appreciates that as each paragraph progresses, the number of readers diminishes. Think of it as an inverted triangle where the number of people who read all the way through to the bottom is always less than those who read the intro. Again, that is not because the news story is badly written or not worthy of inclusion. In fact the exact opposite is true. It is because the journalist is giving the reader the option to stop reading the story as and when they feel that they have absorbed all of the information they require. Indeed, a sub-editor should in theory be able to edit a well written story from the bottom-up without losing anything important from the news story. This is also why article length is not the key attribute that journalists vie for – instead they care about where the story is positioned within the paper. In fact, the best articles and, indeed, the hardest to write are often the shortest. To test this principle for your own

entertainment and, hopefully, inspiration take yourself online or down to the newsagent the next time all of the papers are obliged to lead on the same, complex story – a political story is always good for this little exercise. Then ask yourself who has the harder job as a writer: the broadsheet journalist who has 1,500 words and multiple supporting articles to convey the complex nuances of the story, or the tabloid writer who might only have 150 words and must accurately strip the whole story back so that it can be 'consumed by the masses'?

Now obviously there are more types of article that a journalist must write than just news stories – features, opinion pieces, leaders and sketches all continue to have their place within the news industry. Each has its own writing style and journalistic code. Rather than analysing the writing styles of each, it is more important to appreciate why this mix of articles is required. The answer comes down to sustaining the reader's interest: sketches provide humour, often to dry, political stories; opinion pieces and leaders provide inspiration and convince the reader of the paper's authority and credibility; and, of course, features provide a welcome form of entertainment, inspiration and deeper, more educative reading than the more strait-laced news article will provide. That is not to say that news articles cannot be written in an entertaining style. Open a copy of the Daily

Mail and count up the number of stories that start with a dropped intro to see that engaging the reader is often more important than the story itself. In case you have not come across the term 'dropped intro', it is a writing technique that prevaricates around the focus of the news article within the opening paragraphs in an entertaining way before eventually delivering the actual intro three or more paragraphs into the story.

One final point worth making about the art of news journalism is that this is a style of storytelling that is itself in a state of flux. Many have argued over the last few years that as the attention span of readers gets ever shorter, so the articles must be more concise – a symptom of the Twitter Generation or so people thought. More recently it has become clear that an online news site that only comprises short form articles lacks the level of authority and depth to sustain an audience's interest. That is why you see articles increasing in length and big news stories having more and more supporting stories written around them.

Entertaining Stories

Of course, however engaging a newspaper story is, it is not really a form of entertainment. For that we must turn to the art of storytelling through stage, screen and novel. When you strip all three back, you find that these sorts of stories contain the same raw ingredients for success, insight into which will be vital to any successful content strategy.

Let's begin by covering one of the common discussion points about storytelling within a content strategy, the 'hero's journey'. This is based on the well-trodden premise that there is a core structure to every story whatever its type or origin. Regardless as to whether you subscribe to that theory or not, there are some important points that any content marketing programme should take.

You will instantly see many popular films and books captured within this basic plotline from *Lord of the Rings* to *Star Wars*. Many content marketing experts have overlaid a business language over this hero's journey but a note of gentle caution should be sounded. Remember that it is the customer who is the hero, not your brand! That may seem a ridiculously obvious observation to make, but the danger of storytelling as a company is to easily slip into the trap of creating the story around your brand, product or service. However heroic you may feel as a company, this is going to miss the mark when it comes to audience engagement by a country mile.

HERO'S JOURNEY

ACT 1
Ordinary world
Call to adventure
Refusal of the call
Meeting the mentor
Crossing the threshold

Problems
Challenges
Pain

ACT 2
Tests, allies & enemies
Innermost cave
Ordeal

Solutions

ACT 3
Reward
Road back
Resurrection
Return with elixir

Case Studies

So to make the task of interpreting the hero's journey more straightforward to understand, here is a purposefully dumbed down version using, as a hypothetical example, an innocent marketing director going on a content journey

(the text in brackets is designed to simplify the somewhat colourful language used in the traditional hero's journey into something more applicable within a business context):

Act I – The Journey (i.e. nurturing the audience)

- *Ordinary World (today):* Our marketing director hero has a busy marketing communications programme with a healthy budget for a variety of different activities and campaigns. However, while content is clearly being used there is no deliberate content marketing strategy in place meaning that all of the campaigns and activities are disjointed and focused purely on volume of conversion.

- *Call to Adventure (call to action):* Being an engaged marketing director, our hero becomes increasingly aware of the buzz surrounding content marketing and decides to research further by attending relevant events and reading insight material.

- *Refusal of the Call (fear, uncertainty and doubt):* As the implications of the breadth of change required to adopt a mature content strategy become apparent, and struggling to find practical advice on how to do this, our marketing director hero experiences fear, uncertainty and doubt (the FUD factor) so decides that his marketing communications programme is working fine as it is.

- *Mentor/Sage (proof):* In carrying on with business as usual, our marketing director attends a talk by a member of The Intelligent Marketing Institute, featuring insight into how to align an audience engagement strategy to his existing marketing programme and he turns to the Institute for advice and insight. [Dear reader, we hope you do not mind some gentle humour!]

- *Cross the Threshold (buying threshold):* Our marketing director is persuaded to consider initiating an audience engagement strategy within his company.

Act II – The Transformation (i.e. the buying cycle)

- *Tests & Challenges (consider):* Full on investigation and consideration of what/why and how an audience engagement strategy should be implemented ensues, throwing up a number of tests and challenges that will need to be overcome – e.g. budget constraints, upskilling the team, dealing with IT, managing retained agencies and so the list goes on.

- *Approach to the Centre of Unknown (review):* The plan is now finalised and the various consultancies and agencies that will help deliver the audience engagement strategy are being reviewed. Importantly, internal stakeholder engagement is taking place to align functions that will be impacted.

- *The Ordeal (buy):* It is time to submit the proposal to the board for final approval!

Act III – The Return (i.e. post-purchase and loyalty/retention)

- *The Reward (receive):* Approval has been given and roll out has begun. This involves the complexity of integration across all customer engagement functions.

- *The Road Back (experience):* Success! With the audience engagement strategy live and integrated across all customer engagement functions, the anticipated business outcomes are being realised.

- *Resurrection (acknowledge):* Our marketing director hero now embarks on a storytelling journey internally, ensuring that everyone from the chairman and CEO down realises how these results have been achieved so that the audience engagement strategy becomes an accepted part of business as usual.

- *Return with the Elixir (advocate):* Our marketing director now has a seat on the board and is commonly seen on the speaking circuit, held up as a marketing guru. Fresh career opportunities await!

Reflect upon the above for a moment and you will see that the hero's journey is nothing more than the complete buying cycle – whether the 'thing' you are buying is a product, service or an idea. The difference is that it takes into account the buying cycle from the audience's point of view, not the brand's. You can, in essence, strip the hero's journey back into the following:

Act 1 – Engage the Audience

1. Attract the audience
2. Engage the audience (taking into consideration the FUD factor and need for proof)
3. Reach and cross the threshold

Act 2 – The Buying Cycle

This should represent the buying cycle, which can usually be summarised as:

1. Compare
2. Review
3. Buy

Act 3 – Loyalty, Retention & Advocacy

1. Receive the product/service
2. Experience the product/service
3. Acknowledge success of the product/service
4. Advocate

However, it is worth noting that it is rarely a linear journey nor without complication. To put it in the real world, if you are a consumer considering the purchase of your brand's car, it is unlikely you would rely upon the customer to simply walk into the first showroom they see and buy the first showroom car the showroom is prepared to sell, driving directly home and then enjoying years of trouble free motoring. Life just is not like that. Along the way the customer will experience doubt about whether to buy a new car at all, face delays, compare cars from different brands and the myriad of other common occurrences that happen every day within their buying cycle. Indeed, a lot of the time the journey is never completed, with the prospective customer simply falling out of the funnel or, to use the vernacular within this article, wandering off to take part in a different story.

This is why an effective audience engagement strategy does not simply involve storytelling. The purpose of the audience journey mapping is to encapsulate the fact that your prospective customers will have differing goals and needs, face a range of barriers to purchase, and will need more than simplistic sales messages to end up as customers.

Another thing that the 'hero's journey' overlooks when hailed as the key to the art of storytelling is the wider facets that make a story great. A real hero or heroine within a work of fiction is someone the reader can identify with and ultimately becomes a character that is cared enough about to keep watching or reading. The experiences the hero or heroine faces within the story are vitally important but unless the reader cares about what happens to the character, even if a villain of the piece who the reader longs to see defeated, then they will disengage. The exact same thing applies to any storytelling you do as a company. Unless the stories you are seeking to engage the audience about have a personal appeal enough to make the target audience care, then you will not sustain their interest. That is why the foundation of your content pillars must contain a mix of entertainment, inspiration, education and ability to convince.

Storytelling as a Business

So accepting that storytelling is a fundamental element of a successful audience engagement strategy, then it makes sense to understand how to inject the conditions for great storytelling within your strategy whilst at the same time appreciating the core attributes of great journalism. Therefore, when considering the components that will make up your audience engagement strategy:

- **Identify the aspects of your target audience personas which the story will need to address –**
  - what are their needs/desires/goals/ambitions?
  - what are the barriers that are going to get in the way?
  - what is their attitude and how best to engage with them?
  - who are their influencers?
  - what is the best media to tell the story through?

- **Identify the point of mutuality for each persona, with a story in mind –** when considering what is the central theme that both you as a company and each persona can relate to and engage about, make sure both sides are going to care enough about that point of mutuality so that a compelling story can be told over time; one in which, we must stress, the customer is the hero.

- **Build the content pillars in the same way you would consider the genre from a book or movie –**
  - what will the stories be about?
  - how will they entertain, convince, inspire and educate?
  - what will be within the stories that they can identify with and care about?

- **Map the audience journeys as you would the plot of a book –**
  what is the real buying cycle from the audience's perspective and how does that need to correspond to the thresholds that the prospective customers will need to cross before they buy and are then retained? If you think of these as the 'acts' within the story then you will be able to align all campaigns and activities to the audience progression. How will you ensure you meet their needs/desire/goals/ambitions, overcome their barriers, and stay engaged?

- **Build the editorial calendar with best practice from the world of journalism and within the context of great fiction –**
  if the content pillars and audience journeys are conceived with the art of storytelling at their heart, then the resulting editorial calendar will produce the right sort of content to be delivered through the right sort of channels to engage the audience and achieve your desired business outcome. At the same time, you are not writing a book or making a movie. The story mix from the world of journalism and the practice of great journalistic writing will be essential.

There is No Such Thing as a Reader Any More

Something that novelists, playwrights, poets, directors and scriptwriters do not have to contend with is the active involvement of the reader within their story to the extent that they are as much the writer as you are. However, if you are going to emerge as a brand publisher then you are going to have to contend with the fact that whether the content is on a social media platform or not, your target audience is going to be at liberty to participate in the story creation as much as you are.

In the world of journalism it is a different story, however. The rise of citizen journalists is well understood and where it was once seen as a threat, it is now quite rightly viewed as an extension to the journalist's ability to gather information. Ordinary people with camera phones send 'on the scene footage' that could once only be dreamed of or acquired by sheer happenchance. Think of how iconic the images were of JFK's assassination or the anonymous student protestor who stood fearlessly before a column of tanks in the Tiananmen Square protests of 1989. Should those events be repeated today, then the quantity of footage would be exponentially greater. Brand publishers should be similarly welcoming of such levels of engagement.

At the end of the day, a participating audience is one that is truly engaged. As already outlined in the section entitled 'From Engagement to Participation', nurturing such levels of active involvement is highly advantageous as their interest is more likely to be sustained, they lend the content a patina of independent credibility and they are more likely to act as advocates on your behalf.

Therefore, from a storytelling point of view you are going to have to react flexibly to their involvement. The hero's journey may very well not be in your control. The pace of editorial velocity, which we will refer back to again in a moment, may not be yours to direct. The smart audience strategist will build such flexibility into their planning and react positively when it occurs.

Final Thoughts

Although the art of storytelling should really form a book in its own right, there are a few additional considerations that are worth noting. As a brand publisher trying to engage your audience through great storytelling, there are three words that you should keep front and centre in everything you do:

1. Velocity

Every brand, every target audience and every content pillar will be different in terms of how much content needs delivering every day/week/month. There will be no hard and fast rules that can be applied, but a few things to bear in mind when trying to gauge your own editorial velocity are:

- What resource (time and budget) do you have to support content creation?

- Remember that not all content needs to be created, you can curate it as well.

- Deliver too much content to your audience and it may prove overwhelming, meaning they will switch off because they do not wish to devote the time to keep up.

- Deliver too little content and the audience will get bored and drift away.

- If you try to treat all people in the same way you can also fail, so devise content platforms that allow those who wish to be deeply involved to constantly find more, whilst the less active can skim and be satisfied.

2. Creativity

Just because your content is being delivered through an editorial calendar which has allowed you to cross the chasm to becoming a bona fide brand publisher does not mean that some of the other basic principles of good marketing should be abandoned. Of those, the need for creativity remains paramount.

By being creative in the activities and campaigns you deliver within your content strategy, you will be providing variety, originality and interest for your target audience. This is more likely to ensure they remain engaged and, indeed, become active participants. Obviously this creativity must still be within the context of appropriateness for your brand, your audience and the subject matter.

3. Mutuality

Never forget the key principle that lies within the point of mutuality. Whatever story you try to tell, it must be something that is of mutual interest to your brand and your target audience. If it is not appropriate to your brand then your target audience will not only question why you are producing that content but it also runs the risk of backfiring. If it is not relevant to your target audience you run the risk of failing to engage and simply reverting to broadcasting messages at an unresponsive audience.

Ultimately, becoming a brand publisher is a journey in itself and may seem an alien concept to many. Grasping the fact that to become a brand publisher will also involve engaging in the art of storytelling may feel like a stretch too far. However, to deliver a successful audience engagement strategy you will be obliged to embrace this idea.

In this chapter

B2B Content Marketing

The average B2B marketer has been using content marketing as a key facet of their marketing communications strategy since time immemorial. Compared to their B2C counterparts, the use of thought leadership, conferences, roundtables, newsletters and a myriad of other content-based activities has been fairly standard fare. However, when seeking to transition this existing approach to one that embraces a robust audience engagement strategy, B2B marketers face some stiff and unique challenges.

Arguably the mainstay of B2B content marketing is thought leadership. This approach recognises that touting product or service features and benefits ad nauseam simply does not resonate. Instead, the B2B company must produce content that relates to the business pain-points and opportunities that the target audience currently feels. It is simply far more effective to make your company relevant to the things that are keeping your target audience awake at night than to crow about how wonderful your product or service is.

So ingrained and proven is this approach that the overwhelming majority of B2B PR campaigns and a sizeable proportion of marketing activities revolve around thought leadership. However, generally speaking where such content-based activity fits within the audience engagement mix is poorly understood.

The reality is that thought leadership is an excellent tool within pre-funnel audience engagement activity. In other words, before any sense of sales engagement is begun, thought leadership is the primary tool for drawing the audience towards the brand. Once the sales cycle has begun, the effectiveness of thought leadership tapers off. This is not the weakness of thought leadership as an approach, but because a normal sales team lives in a siloed, bonus-driven bubble where it does not occur to the sales rep to tap the marketing communications team on the shoulder to produce the sort of content that would help them as they progress the sale. When a sale can last anywhere from six to eighteen months, this lack of integration is a shameful oversight.

When the opposite approach is taken, the results can be staggering. As just one isolated example where the authors can speak from personal experience, when Chordiant, a B2B technology company, had its eyes firmly set on winning Lloyds TSB it took the unique step of integrating all sales, marketing and communications with staggering effectiveness. By identifying the key buyers and influencers at the bank, and as insights into their pains and needs came to light, so thought leadership content was produced specifically for those target people. This content was then activated through the channels those targets would consume: press, direct marketing, events and so on – given it was 2008, this was before B2B social media could be used as an effective channel. The end result was the deal brought comfortably to fruition. Sadly, such examples are few and far between.

It should also be noted that thought leadership is equally powerful for ongoing customer engagement. To be a successful B2B company tends to imply there are excellent Customer Relationship Management systems and practices in place to aid retention and expose cross-sell and up-selling opportunities. Providing genuinely useful content to your customers is therefore a powerful tool for maintaining that relationship.

The Journey From Thought Leadership to a Content Strategy

One of the strengths of existing B2B content marketing is that it has a natural tendency to build itself around the audience. In other words, the content is already designed to tap into the audience's interests and to be relevant.

However, due to the siloed nature of some businesses, more often than not the thought leadership stands in isolation. This means that the audience is not taken on a journey, largely because there is a lack of appreciation of what an audience journey looks like. If you do a rough sketch of each customer-facing silo, then the customer relationship managers are handed over a customer for project delivery and ongoing customer support. Sales have received that lead from marketing and as far as they are concerned, the role of marketing is simply to deliver those leads to the sales team to qualify and then manage through the prolonged sales cycle. What is important to note is that in handing over that lead, it is simply the contact details and information gleaned from the prospect that is handed over. There is no attempt to consider what the content journey for that prospect might have been. Finally, while marketing and communications are more likely to be integrated within a B2B organisation than in a B2C business, the outbound campaigns and activities are often disjointed.

An appreciation of an audience journey within a content strategy would help break down these silos. Although, it is also worth pointing out that a content strategy will not work effectively unless those silos are broken down.

Consider each customer-facing function from a linear audience journey perspective and consider who will be involved within each aspect of that artificially linear journey:

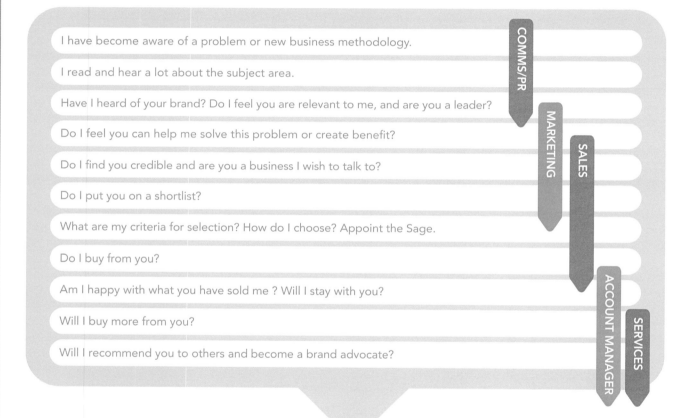

I have become aware of a problem or new business methodology.

I read and hear a lot about the subject area.

Have I heard of your brand? Do I feel you are relevant to me, and are you a leader?

Do I feel you can help me solve this problem or create benefit?

Do I find you credible and are you a business I wish to talk to?

Do I put you on a shortlist?

What are my criteria for selection? How do I choose? Appoint the Sage.

Do I buy from you?

Am I happy with what you have sold me ? Will I stay with you?

Will I buy more from you?

Will I recommend you to others and become a brand advocate?

COMMS/PR

MARKETING

SALES

ACCOUNT MANAGER

SERVICES

Now, overlay that with a more plausible audience engagement story arc that reflects more closely how the target audience will behave:

Act I – The Nurturing

- *Ordinary World:* Multitude of headaches and business opportunities, but possibly lack of awareness or understanding of how the B2B company could be of help.

- *Engagement:* Content engages the prospect to identify the B2B company as understanding their pain/needs.

- *Resistance:* The bumpy road in turning the engagement into a two-way conversation.

- *Influence:* The crucial role third party influencers play in providing credibility and endorsement.

- *Crossing the Threshold:* Success of all of the above will be measured by securing a meeting.

Act II – The Purchasing

- *Consider:* The cut and thrust of the sales cycle.

- *Review:* Not just the review of your product/service but of your competitors; this would also include bid submission and review.

- *Buy:* The negotiations, if successful bidder.

Act III – The Experiencing

- *Receive:* Delivery/implementation/execution of the product/service.

- *Experience:* One received/live, the actual experience of the product/service and the measurement of success.

- *Acknowledge:* The path to advocacy must pass from experience success through acknowledging the benefits the product/service has brought.

- *Advocate:* The ultimate achievement is to turn the customer into an advocate and so help you grow your business further.

Be advised that whilst the above may seem linear, in reality the target audience could linger at any stage and go backwards and forwards somewhat anarchically as the prospect slowly crawls towards becoming a customer and then an advocate. However, it should clearly show how an audience engagement strategy that is understood and deployed by all customer-facing functions is going to provide greater chance of engagement and coherence for the prospect and customer. Such audience alignment will provide powerful results.

But those results will be marred if the audience is not correctly understood. It is a well-known fact that B2B companies are very neglectful when it comes to audience insight and research. It is not that the knowledge does not exist within the organisation, it is that this knowledge resides in people's heads and is not fleshed out and codified into personas that everyone can understand and benefit from using. If B2B companies were to invest in some market research to confirm these insights, then the businesses would stand a far better chance of engaging a greater proportion of the potential customer base.

The Role of Creativity in a B2B Audience Engagement Strategy

A recent trend within B2B marketing and communications has been the activation of creative campaigns that are very much B2C in their approach. In other words, not only do these campaigns employ the sort of creativity that is par for the course for a B2C brand, but the campaign itself is delivered through B2C channels.

The spark for this trend has been the ever-increasing challenges B2B brands have faced when it comes to differentiating themselves and capturing their audience's attention. What this trend highlights is that B2B brands are also beginning to think about their target audiences beyond simply their job titles and instead considering them more as individuals. The traditional approach of taking out some limited advertising space in airports with the aim of targeting the business traveller has now extended itself to thinking of the target decision-maker as a person who exists within a multi-media world.

This is the start of the journey to building more complete audience personas and will provide powerful insights for a B2B brand. Such insights, when delivered through an audience engagement strategy, will enable the brand to become more relevant, personable and attractive. This is because a mature audience engagement strategy will balance the need to sustain the engagement with the target audience through the many months of an end-to-end sales cycle – and by this we are referring to beginning with awareness raising, through to converting the prospect into a customer and then finally into a brand advocate – with the need for campaigns. And as those campaigns will be designed to deliver the content pillars, then the B2B brand will be trying to find the correct balance between the drier foundation layers of educating and convincing with the more energetic need to entertain and inspire. The need for creativity therefore becomes apparent.

Of course, such conundrums have always faced any B2B brand that targets an SME audience. That no doubt explains why SME marketing communications programmes are often at the cutting edge of content-led marketing. Intuit, a provider of software for small businesses, is a prime example of this.

When, in 2008/9, Intuit sought to massively invest in the UK and to grow its small business user base, it deployed a well-conceived 'Win On The Web' strategy. To support that, a content marketing programme was activated that was designed to connect with UK small businesses, whatever sector or region the business was in. The result was the Small Business Britain website (since rolled into another engagement platform by Intuit) that engaged small businesses about key issues of the day, such as the Budget and the 2010 General Election. The success of the campaign was down to its ability to connect with small business owners about issues that were relevant to them as businesspeople and that they would wish to take time to engage in. The mix of content, such as research, opinion, guides and commentary, delivered over several marketing communications channels, was ideal for the target audience group. So successful was the campaign in engaging audiences, elevating the brand and driving traffic, that Intuit replicated the approach globally.

The Wider Benefits of a Content Strategy

It should also be noted that there are several benefits that an audience engagement strategy approach will bring to a B2B business that are not realised today:

- **Demonstrable ROI:** proving return on investment within B2B marketing communications has always been challenging. When the campaign is oriented towards lead generation then the marketing director is usually in safe territory. However, tracking wider business objectives around brand engagement, PR ROI, customer engagement and the myriad of other activities that fall within the remit of the marketing department is not so easy. A content-led approach should, therefore, have tremendous appeal to a B2B marketing director because business outcomes are more easily tracked and measured.

- **Content insight:** by activating a content-led marketing approach, the company becomes a brand publisher with the reader being your business's reader and not just a reader via a third party publisher. This approach continues to face the criticism from certain quarters that the target audience will not find a B2B brand publisher credible, authoritative and independent. However, that is because the 'point of mutuality' is not defined and the content marketing programme is still in a message broadcast mode rather than seeking genuine audience engagement and participation.

- **End to the leaky funnel:** as described elsewhere, a successful audience engagement strategy sustains the engagement with all prospects and customers, not simply those who progress through the sales funnel. For the huge percentage that do not progress within any given campaign, the audience engagement strategy maintains their interest and ensures that they can be easily fed into any subsequent campaign. Of course some prospects will decline to engage, but the lost percentage will be significantly less than in a normal marketing campaign.

- **Easier to sustain:** it is often the case with thought leadership programmes that B2B brands find it hard to sustain a regular output – feeding the thought leadership machine is a perpetual challenge. The rigour around the planning elements of an audience engagement strategy mitigates this challenge to such an extent that it should never prove a problem again.

- **Role of the marketing function:** as already mentioned above, an effective audience engagement strategy will align all customer facing functions within the company. However, it also elevates the role of marketing because, as the guardian of the content strategy and therefore all audience engagement, the marketing function's relevance and control over the success metrics radically changes its role within the business.

The Elephant in the Room

Of course, the road to adopting a content-led approach to customer engagement within a B2B company will not be without its challenges. For a start, most B2B marketing communications functions are relatively modest in size, both in terms of resource and budget. As such, proving the internal business case will face considerable scrutiny.

There is no one-size-fits-all answer to this challenge. However, there are several points that need to be made which should help overcome these hurdles.

First of all, for the vast majority of B2B businesses the move to a content-led approach should be an evolution not a revolution. Most B2B companies are already doing thought leadership and other core components will be in place to a greater or lesser degree. While the structure will need to be built and upfront investment will be required to fulfil the content strategy alignment with the existing marketing communications programme, this is not about starting with a blank sheet of paper.

Secondly, although existing activities and campaigns will now be directed by the content strategy, their nature need not necessarily change. If they are fit for purpose as vehicles for delivering the content then there is certainly no need for change for change's sake. However, the 'sustain' element of the audience engagement strategy may need to be built from scratch or involve amending the way in which sustained communications activities, such as social media, are driven.

The third point is regarding the content itself. Many B2B companies are concerned about the resource requirements to create the necessary volume of content. It must therefore be noted that there are excellent tools already available that will enable the curation of content to work instead of or, more likely, alongside created content.

Finally, it is perfectly feasible to develop and improve the audience engagement strategy over time, so that as the business case is proven so investment can be justified. In fact, for mature B2B companies with an established brand and customer base, such a steady transition will almost certainly be preferable in terms of taking your audience and advocates on the journey with you.

The Rise of Video Content

Video occupies a unique and special place in human society and modern history. For more than half a century iconic moments have been captured, communicated and remembered through video; be it wars and revolutions through to royal weddings and royal births. Today video is a mainstream media commodity, capturing the attention of millions of people every day through YouTube, online news channels and more. Therefore any marketing communications strategy that ignores video is one that is potentially doomed to failure.

In fact, so essential is video as a content media that it is somewhat odd to have to point this out. However, from a brand publishing point of view, the use of video is often very immature and fixed around a few approaches, usually as a standalone element of a campaign. Yet when the wider perspective is taken, comparing the use of video within the world of online news, then it becomes easier to understand why there is so far still to go.

Video Today

Any discussion about video has to start with an analysis of YouTube. Of all the social media platforms, it is easy to argue that YouTube has the greatest chance of standing the test of time. This is simply because it has carved out a distinct and simple niche as **the** ubiquitous video sharing platform and it is very hard to see why it would ever fall out of favour with users. If someone is looking for a video, then it is assumed that it will be hosted on YouTube. And that now extends to entire YouTube channels existing, providing a new and unique platform for the broadcasting of video.

Use of YouTube by brands has naturally been quite extensive. Take, for example, Coca-Cola. As a brand, Coke has a very mature approach to content marketing and, indeed, so confident is it that you can take a look at its content strategy through videos the company has posted on YouTube – just search on YouTube for 'Coke Content 2020'. From a consumer perspective, you will find a raft of engaging content depending on your interests. Examples include: Coke Studio (video music channel), Coca-Cola (adverts channel), and the many ads designed around specific campaigns, such as 'Coca-Cola Happiness Machine', 'Share a Coke' and 'Celebrate London 2012'.

And then, of course, there is YouTube's place in the world of viral videos. Obviously you cannot simply create a viral video. Great videos go viral of their own accord (although you can give them some firm nudges to get them going!) and whilst there are certain ingredients that can trigger the viral spread of a video, it is an absolute given that for every video that does go viral there are dozens that fail to do so. The best viral videos are not simply those that entertain – such as Coke Zero Skyfall or the Dutch Channel's TNT's 'A Dramatic Surprise on a Quiet Square'. Instead, success is typically more widely measured by its ability to communicate brand messages, such as the Tipp-Ex 'Hunter Shoots a Bear', or Volvo's Van Damme 'Epic Split Stunt'.

It would be remiss, however, not to mention the darker side of video. Like any content, video can potentially do a brand as much harm as it does good and as wonderful as YouTube is as a platform for enabling your target audience to see your great video content, that same audience can also view any other content about your brand that may be posted. Keeping with Coca-Cola, here is a case in point. Any searches for the brand on YouTube will show numerous videos about Coke that have been created and posted by ordinary people. Some are neutral in tone, such as the curiously explosive experiments that can be conducted with fizzy drinks. Others are potentially more harmful.

YouTube is not, of course, the only social media video platform; however, it is the most ubiquitous. It is also, one would argue, not so much a social media platform as a content platform; as much a medium for content as Freesat or Sky. And whilst it is dominant, it is far from alone when it comes to the hosting of video content. Its main rival is online video news.

You Saw it Here First

Since the dawn of cinema, the moving picture has become the dominant form of news media. Text and photo simply cannot compete when it comes to conveying a news story. Wars, for example, have become epitomised by the viewer's ability to watch and hear the events on a foreign battlefield; a phenomena which is in no way new, by the way, as a film of the Battle of the Somme in the First World War, admittedly made by the British Government, was viewed in cinemas by an astonishing twenty million people in just six weeks. However, now we expect images from any conflict to be beamed into our living rooms or onto our PCs, smartphones or tablets, and for it to be live and 24/7; this may be something that we now take for granted but just thirty years ago during the Falklands War, news video footage was taking two weeks or longer to reach newsrooms in the UK. And it is not just wars, conflicts and civil unrest that receive saturated 'always on' treatment with anything from a royal baby birth (well, the image of the hospital entrance anyway) to the selection of the Pope (white smoke drifting from a chimney) being witnessed by millions live in all its drawn out high definition glory.

The reality is that video news is going through its own revolution at the moment. Online is changing everything. A recent (2013) pioneering piece of research conducted by Deloitte on behalf of The Associated Press proves this. Already half as many people (in the UK) will turn to the internet when a story breaks as will turn on their TV, and in total nearly two-thirds will turn to video content for a breaking news story – and bear in mind this is any breaking news story, not just those that could be considered visually dramatic. Where online truly comes into its own is when it comes to additional information. As the report points out: 'websites were the most popular source of additional information on a breaking news story. The popularity of websites as a secondary source extends across all ages, although it is most pronounced with younger age groups. In the UK more than half of over 65s, who have the highest average consumption of TV, use websites to get more detail on a breaking story. Among 16–24s, the proportion rises to seven out of ten who choose a website compared with just 37% for TV.'

The insights from the Deloitte/AP research come thick and fast. It clearly demonstrated that 'video enhances the online news experience, adding colour and animating stories in a way that is difficult to achieve with text alone' adding that 'among those respondents who had watched news video online, the majority told us that it brought a story to life and improved their understanding, as well as making the news easier to follow.' The clear point here is that most content marketing today relies on text; a factor that is not helped by using content platforms that have been or in many cases still are restrictive when it comes to video, be it the common social media platforms, e-mail or even a print publication. What the research showed is not that text-based content, from a news perspective, is obsolete but that users tended to find it quicker to watch a video than read text online with the research stating 'that the appeal of video lies more in its ability to add depth to online news stories, rather than in replacing text.'

No wonder, then, that the research found that 86% of UK respondents used online news sources frequently and 61% claimed to have watched news video clips on a regular basis. This clearly demonstrates the readiness of people to engage with content through video. Indeed, the research concluded that 'video is no longer a luxury add-on to a professional news site: it is becoming an essential part of the news experience for consumers. Not only does video increase loyalty and differentiate between services, it enables news organisations to engage with the YouTube Generation in a way that text-based websites, newspapers and TV do not.'

The Deloitte/AP research proved the case for broadcasters, traditional print media publishers and any online news outlet to invest in online video content if they want to capture and retain audiences. For content marketers it should act as a wake-up call, showing that whatever content is created or curated, its effectiveness will be limited if video is not embedded at the heart of the strategy.

Things Will Only Get Better For Video

If the importance of video is rising today, it will be an absolute given tomorrow. The fact is that the younger generation simply expect video content as a given. Back to the Deloitte/AP research: '71% of UK 16–24s considers video essential to a good news website or app, compared with an average of 49% across all age groups. If video is important for driving this age group to a news site, it is just as important for getting them to click on a given story. 68% of 16–24s said that they would be more likely to click on a story that they knew contained video, rather than one that had text only.' Whilst that research may have been referring to news, it is as relevant for any form of content.

Advances in technology are also going to support the rise of video content. Already in recent years the ability for technology to support video consumption has improved dramatically. Smartphones, tablets, 3G and now 4G, and better broadband connectivity have made it far easier to download, access and view video content anywhere and anytime. Clearly, future advances will amplify this trend further.

Implications for the Content Marketer

As already stated, the most resounding implication for the content marketer is that video content must be deemed as vital as text, photo or image-based content – the latter has not been referred to so far but clearly imagery in the form of presentations (such as those accessed through SlideShare) or infographics has an equally valid role to play depending on the target audience. However, the challenge lies in how to tell stories through video and, most importantly, to swap between text, video, photo and image when telling a sustained story.

On this point it is worth considering the lessons already learnt by the online news sites. Take, for example, the BBC news online site. Already the site has transitioned from a siloed state where videos sat to one side of the text stories, to today where they are blended in within the story package. If you want to access a news story, you can do so by reading the text, clicking on videos, or a blend of the two within the story. However, the experience is not seamless. While the text may refer to an embedded video package this is by no means the norm and certainly there is little evidence that the video packages are being specifically commissioned to stitch a single story together. This is probably the direction the BBC will take in time but would, of course, involve restructuring the way news is gathered; at the moment the online editors have to make use of video material that is being made by the various BBC news teams around the world, as well as their news agency feeds. A content marketer should not face such limitations when planning their editorial calendar.

When it comes to the storytelling itself, the important thing to do is to suppress the instinct to treat video as either a creative tool or an expensive luxury. Of course video can still be used as a creative campaign tool but at the same time it must be an everyday part of the content process. As just one example, if your campaign needs audience reviews then make sure you build in the ability to gather those as video reviews as well as text-based reviews. In relation to the content pillars, videos can play as integral a role as text, photos or images when it comes to the foundation of entertaining, educating, inspiring or convincing. So whatever the actual content pillars you deploy, video can be used.

Where that video content comes from is a different challenge. Curation platforms for video content are few and far between and the industry is yet to gear itself up to provide a wide pool of videographers that are easy to find and engage. This will come in time, though, and will be accessible through the Power Crowd, for example.

Then there is the question of using video as a means of engagement. If the goal is audience participation, then this is easily done through text and photo, but video may be perceived as a barrier to engagement. Will your target audience create and submit a video and even if they do, is the quality going to be satisfactory? This is despite the fact that video recording has never been easier thanks to the proliferation of cameras on smartphones and the fact that virtually all modern digital cameras allow for video recording. Natural technological evolution may, of course, answer this question. After all, advances in modern cameras have meant that it has never been easier to take a good quality photo; the same will no doubt apply to video one day. However, the more immediate answer has already been proven through the successful examples of interactive video content. Take, for example, the Tipp-Ex 'Hunter Shoots a Bear' viral mentioned earlier. This brilliantly conceived viral video is in reality a montage of video clips which lets the user define what to watch with highly amusing consequences.

The final point that must be made with regards to video content is the common weakness seen within most brand videos today. For some reason the idea of digital journeys has not yet sunk in. Great videos, such as the Van Damme 'Epic Split Stunt' for Volvo, lacks any form of easy-to-follow link for the viewer. As a result, a huge proportion of the audience is lost as it is reliant on the viewer proactively Googling and taking themselves to the Volvo website to watch other videos from that campaign or, more importantly, learn more about the trucks – the entire point of the video in the first place. Not only does this mean lost audience, as so commonly happens, but it also means that Volvo is missing a massive trick in being able to sustain the engagement in different ways with the different personas. An intelligent content strategy approach would have plotted different journeys from that single viral video for fleet managers, truck drivers, Volvo brand advocates, and so on.

So the overarching message has to be to embrace video because your audiences have already embraced video and will continue to do so. At the same time, recognise that video is not standalone content but is just another form of content within your audience engagement strategy; appreciate that new thinking is required if video is going to integrated successfully; and finally, view video as an excellent way of engaging your audience in a way that evidence shows will create greater levels of sustained engagement.

SECTION

4

Capabilities & Architecture

In section 3 we walked you through the theory and thinking part of creating your engagement strategy. You are probably asking how that is now put into practice. This section is about the practicalities. It is not straightforward, as you may have already worked out, as there are a number of 'moving' parts. What we mean by moving parts is that some of what we are about to describe is our future vision of what you will be able to do once some of the functions become automated through technology. However, you **can** still implement your audience engagement strategy without these technologies.

In fact, the first task is down to your creative brainpower. Creating your engagement strategy plan is about designing and building your personas, points of mutuality, content pillars and journey maps as we have described in section 3. This will involve getting your organisation aligned to this new way of working. Within this section we have provided templates and structures that will help you focus on what you need without having to worry about the 'how' of delivery at the beginning. In each chapter we will provide you with the manual workaround until the technology is available – something we are entirely confident will happen very soon. Chapter 7 has a staged plan that will help you through the implementation.

In section 2, chapter 3 we introduced the capabilities architecture for the components of ICE. Each chapter in this section will describe those capabilities in more detail. As a start point in each chapter we have described the basic functionality of the capabilities as you may not be familiar with these tools. We focus on three capabilities; campaign management, Decision Engines and marketing resource management.

Each of these chapters will then describe how these existing technologies should be integrated for the ICE architecture. This is our future vision.

Implementing ICE can be done in stages and you can work with your existing capabilities. You may look at the architecture diagram and feel that there are things missing; most notably social marketing is not shown. However, no channels are specifically listed and we have simply said either inbound or outbound. The first reason that we have not listed any channel-specific capability is that this is a constantly evolving space and all the larger vendors tend to add new capability as it becomes necessary. Secondly, ICE is about 'what' you are going to deliver and not 'how' you are going to deliver it. We have highlighted inbound and outbound as different as the tools in these areas work in different and very specific ways that we covered in section 2 chapter 3. Outbound and inbound are distinct within the audiences' context.

Just so you don't have to flick back here is the architecture diagram again:

We will start at the top of this diagram and work our way down through the following chapters.

SUMMARY

A fully optimised and integrated engagement strategy will require technology advancements. However, you **can** start to build and implement your engagement strategy straight away.

There is a clear need for automation as this will provide significant improvements in the success of the communications, but it will also affect the speed at which you can learn what works and adapt accordingly.

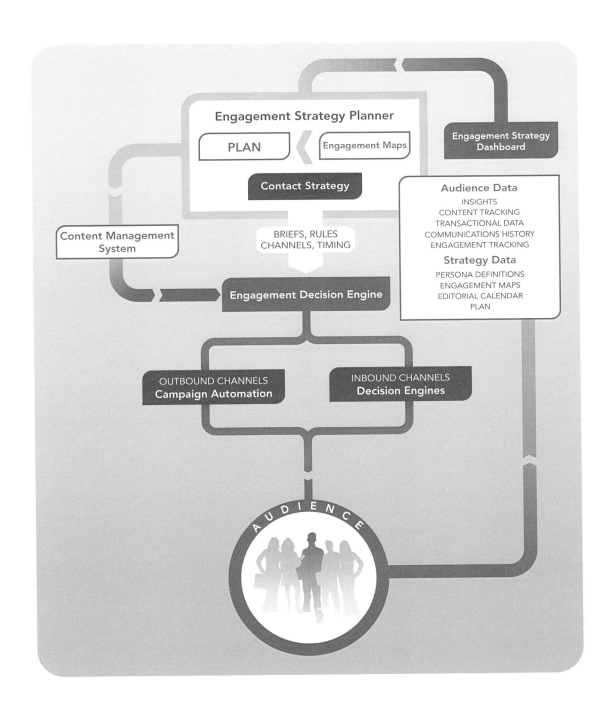

In this chapter

- Persona Definitions
- Content Pillars
- Engagement Maps

Engagement Strategy Planner

The first task, as we described in the previous chapter, is to design the components of your audience engagement strategy as we have put forward in section 3. Starting at the top of the capabilities architecture model, then, is the Engagement Strategy Planner.

The purpose of the Engagement Strategy Planner is to document your audience engagement strategy and then to use it to create your plan and the briefs for the content and other communications. You will also be able to manage and monitor the plan from this capability.

Manual Workaround

MW

As mentioned, many of the capabilities need automation if they are going to run efficiently and most effectively. However, the lack of automation today is by no means a barrier to progressing with the execution of your audience engagement strategy. In the case of the Engagement Strategy Planner, you can build the maps in a spreadsheet – a template is used below in the examples. In order to demonstrate how to complete it we are going to run through setting up an audience engagement strategy for a bank.

Defining Personas

The first challenge you will face is defining which personas you are targeting. To do this you will need to start with the information and insights that you already have at your disposal. When analysing this insight, you are seeking to identify differences that could mean that any given audience needs to be communicated with using different content and in different ways. At first this will involve identifying all possible persona permutations, especially as they relate to different attitudes that your target audiences will have. However, what you will soon realise is that no matter how much the personas differ on paper, when it comes to defining the engagement maps you will find that multiple personas can be tagged to individual maps. This obviously reduces the number of engagement maps you will be using with the positive by-product of reducing the complexity by several orders of magnitude. Revert to section 3, chapter 1 for the things to think about in defining your personas.

Please note that we know that segmentation data is not necessarily the right information that you need to build the personas; however, often that is all that you have access to. So, in the spirit of 'we are where we are' we will use the existing segmentation data as the point where we start aligning what you are already doing with our audience engagement strategy. From your existing segment information and insights, you need to determine if each segment is one persona or if your personas will go across multiple segments.

In section 3, chapter 3 we discussed content pillars and what the pillar needs to be able to do. A key point we made is that the content pillar will be linked to a goal and that if it does not meet the criteria we have defined for a content pillar it is unlikely to achieve that goal. As you will hopefully have gathered, the setting of these goals is a key difference between an ordinary content strategy and a far more mature audience engagement strategy. We now go a little further and dig deeper into the journey as it is mapped for the pillar as this is essential information you will require when defining your personas.

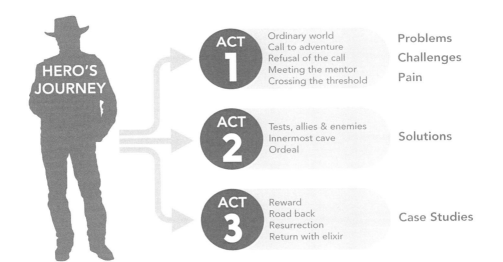

HERO'S JOURNEY

ACT 1
Ordinary world
Call to adventure
Refusal of the call
Meeting the mentor
Crossing the threshold

Problems
Challenges
Pain

ACT 2
Tests, allies & enemies
Innermost cave
Ordeal

Solutions

ACT 3
Reward
Road back
Resurrection
Return with elixir

Case Studies

In discussing the hero's journey in previous chapters you will have seen that at the end of Act 1, the audience (our hero) needs to *'cross the threshold'*. This threshold is the emotional barrier that the audience is crossing towards being interested in purchasing whatever you are selling; but it is also a threshold that you cross as an organisation. It is where you become more connected to the audience. This is most likely where you cross the 'line', from above the line to below the line. It means that you will be able to use more direct communication methods and capabilities. The goal of crossing the threshold is not usually in a content strategy. For example, take a look at the Volvo Trucks YouTube video with Jean Claude Van Damme. It is a great video but if I am a fleet buyer of trucks how do I follow this through on the Volvo website for more information to buy? I crossed the threshold as a buyer but Volvo were not there to meet me.

The problem is that where most content strategies currently sit is in Act 1. This is because they generally have 'softer' goals which are usually about creating an audience, but not much more. This is not the fault of the agencies creating the content who are simply performing to the brief they have been given. Instead this is a silo problem. Brand marketing, communications or marketing are creating a brief that is then not connected to below the line campaigns and sales processes. This is a sweeping statement and you may have different labels for these departments, but we have found that these sorts of disconnections are commonplace.

So, our goals are not just to gather an audience and then 'engage' with them. To us, engagement means crossing the threshold – i.e. not simply the common use of the word 'engagement' where someone merely 'liked' you on Facebook! Our goals are hard business numbers that we can prove and be accountable for achieving. After all, lack of accountability and good measurement also seems to be a common state for many ordinary content strategies. Therefore, when analysing your personas you are not simply looking at where they are starting from, but equally importantly what the threshold needs to be for each persona.

For the example that we are working through our goals are to:

- sell the target audience a mortgage; and

- make sure that we retain the target audience as customers as they go through some key life events.

Dinkys

Category	
Work:	Skilled manual workers, mid-management.
Family:	No children.
Earnings:	Mid to high earnings bracket, enjoy luxury items.
Interests:	Skiing, gourmet food, wine, fashion, sport and DIY.
Entertainment & Readership:	Their choice of newspaper tends to be The News of the World or The Sunday Sport.
Cars:	2 cars bought new or nearly new.
Finance:	Mortgage, pension and may have other savings plans.
Technology:	Always have the latest gadgets and toys.
Internet:	Regularly use the internet for research, entertainment and shopping. Are likely to bank online.

Working parents

Category	
Work:	Skilled tradesman/manual workers.
Family:	2 or more children.
Earnings:	Lower earnings bracket.
Interests:	DIY is one of the favourites.
Entertainment & Readership:	They read tabloid newspapers like The Sun, The Star and The News of the World and they enjoy watching television via satellite.
Cars:	2 family cars bought second hand.
Finance:	Life assurance, child savings plan, own their home with a mortgage.
Technology:	Not laggards, but don't always buy the latest big thing. Technology has to perform a function, it's not just entertainment.
Internet:	Research products and prices and tend to purchase low cost items online such as CDs, DVDs, video games and books.

Insights and research on our segments:

Spend, spend, spend...

Category	
Work:	Office/clerical worker, skilled tradesmen or in education/medical profession.
Family:	This couple tend to be between the ages of 45-54 with 2 or more older children that are still living at home. Married or divorced.
Earnings:	Mid-earnings bracket, live slightly beyond their means.
Interests:	DIY, hiking, walking, cycling and surfing the web. (Not interested in the environment.)
Entertainment & Readership:	They tend not to read a newspaper.
Cars:	2 or more.
Finance:	Typically they have 3 credit cards, but rarely pay off the balance and have no large investments for the future. They will have a mortgage.
Technology:	Keen to keep up with technology, they own games consoles, iPods, and satellite or cable TV.
Internet:	Research as well as purchasing music, books and IT equipment.

Professional Families

Category	
Work:	Self-employed or work as senior managers.
Family:	2 or more children of all ages living in privately owned detached houses.
Earnings:	High earnings bracket.
Interests:	They care about the environment plus have a wide range of hobbies, from sport and exercise to gourmet food, eating out, foreign travel and current affairs.
Entertainment & Readership:	The Times and The Sunday Times, satellite TV, frequently eat out.
Cars:	At least 2, one likely to be a company car. They favour Audi, Land Rover, Mercedes and Saab.
Finance:	Mortgage, many credit cards, savings, investments, and pensions.
Technology:	As you might expect the latest of everything.
Internet:	Much of their purchasing is done online. In fact they are the group that were the early adopters for buying their groceries via the internet, most likely from Ocado.

A word of warning, you must be able to identify these different personas within your data if you are going to communicate directly with them (outbound) and in a way that is specific for the persona. The risk here is that otherwise your content may miss the mark. For inbound, you will find that the audience is self-selecting as to which persona they are **if** your content has been written appropriately for the audience.

If we were considering this from the traditional approach to marketing, we would design a campaign for the product (a mortgage) and all these different people would get more or less the same message. Given the goal we have set, that might be the easier approach which means you can just do a one-size-fits-all campaign. The problem is that those methods are now failing as our audiences have learnt to put these messages straight in the bin, delete them or ignore them if they are adverts. If your message is not directly appealing to me by being of interest and engaging now and not just trying to sell me something, then I will not even read it.

There are quite a few differences between each of the groups of people we outlined above and in the real world you may have a lot more segments than this. The first rule, though, is to find out whether you have the data to identify these people on your marketing systems. You can only use what you have but you still might be able to do a great deal with a lot less than we have described here. For the purpose of this exercise, we will assume our bank has this data so we can separate them. These differences are important as they give us different start points for the journey that we want the target audiences to go on and this will impact the type of content received and the way it is delivered. However, as we will see when we develop the audience engagement maps, the content/stories may merge at the later stages. You will find this happens quite frequently as you develop your audience engagement strategy which is why we are using these examples.

The following table will show how the persona gets developed and what we need to know to get to the next stage of the audience engagement strategy:

Segment	Start Point	Needs/Pains/Goals	Barriers
Dinkys	First home together, just on the property ladder. Not considering the bank at all.	Want to get to the next rung on the ladder and get a larger property to start a family. Would be good to make other property investments now as well as our home.	Life is comfortable as it is now, don't need to move right away. Why move when we have life's luxuries? Getting the next mortgage will be hard now that we have to sell first and will be in a chain.
Working Parents	Been with the same bank for years, not always the best experience but changing is more trouble than it is worth.	Would like to extend the house to get a little more room, can't move as that would be too expensive.	We are getting by as we are, no need to change the status quo, don't want to take on any more debt.
Spend, Spend, Spend	Bank is just in the long list of where to get money, can't see the difference between them.	Would like to help the children get their own places and downsize our home so they can't come back!	Got too much debt as it is and need to pay down our credit cards first.
Professional Families	Happy with my bank, been with them for years.	Would like to extend my investments into property as a landlord.	Don't really have time to invest in property and become a landlord.

Segment	Influencers	Attitude	Purchase Trigger Points
Dinkys	Yahoo finance, friends, family.	Banks are to be battled with to get your mortgage. It's difficult to get a mortgage so you go with who the broker can get you.	Right property becomes available. Ease of application process. A process that would make moving easier (chain).
Working Parents	The papers, friends, family.	Won't be able to top up the mortgage so why even think about it?	Top-up process was easy and we could consolidate other debt into our mortgage and reduce our monthly payments overall.
Spend, Spend, Spend	Research online, friends, family.	Have too much debt to consider anything else.	If we could downsize and sort our finances in one go that would be great.
Professional Families	The Financial Times, financial advisor, family.	Don't have time for this at the moment.	If investments in property could be made 'low touch' where I just make the investments and someone else does the work.

From the information that we have above, we can see that we do in fact have four different personas as this is defined by their start points, their goals and therefore which content pillars they are more likely to engage with. However, when you are looking at your existing segmentation you may find that your personas do not match neatly to your segments, but only by breaking them down with this sort of analysis will you be able to work this out.

We have captured attitude as one straight statement in the above table; however, in reality you will want to know about a number of different attitudes. The following table gives you an example of what these attitudes might be for our example and the 'heat map' represents the position that an individual might have. You can make an educated guess at this but ideally you would undertake research on your personas to determine what the average heat map looks like. This is important as it gives you the start point for your journey but also clarifies the challenge you have in getting your audience over the first threshold – in essence, it creates permutations on each persona. For your content strategy to be successful it has to be able to take the audience over the thresholds or you will not achieve the business outcomes that you are looking for.

Attitude to...	Negative	Neutral	Positive
Bank		▓	
Innovation			
Mortgage purchase	▓		
Home Management		▓	
Home Improvement		▓	
Investments			
Risk & Security			

Mutuality

The point of mutuality (POM), as defined in section 3 chapter 1, is not necessarily defined from the brand, it may be defined between your audience and any of the following:

- Product

- Goal

- Brand Value(s)

- Sponsorship

For our example, we are going to define just one POM from the goal and product: mortgages. Our point of mutuality is therefore 'property'. However, in looking at the research there are others we could use such as:

- **Security** – Planning for the future

- **Risk Management** – Protection of assets

- **Money Management** – 'Super scrimpers', not talking about bank products but more general money saving and planning ideas. However, this might also cover things like managing the household budget and creating a budget in the first place.

In an ideal world, you will test the point of mutuality through research. However, many brands have already gained a clear understanding of what will work, just never chosen to use it. Ultimately, the decision is down to you as to whether you feel research is required or not but bear in mind that changing the point of mutuality is one of the single most hard things to do within an audience engagement strategy. At the same time, a considerable amount of investment will go into generating the platforms and content to support the point of mutuality.

Content Pillars

Now that we have the point of mutuality identified, the content pillars can be defined by referring back to the research that we have for our personas.

Our content pillars for the bank are:

- Property Investment

- Extending & Renovating

- Moving Home

- Becoming a Landlord

These content pillars must enable us to take the story across the first threshold to get the audience engaged and then in the mindset to consider buying. If we do not do that, we are only satisfying our need to create engagement that does not actually lead to any improved business. This is the problem with many social marketing efforts, getting 100k likes on Facebook does not mean they like you now or are engaged. Even if they are commenting on Facebook, if the audience does not move forward past this, it is pointless. For example, the 2014 World Cup saw a massive competition between brands to engage audiences through social media. Very, very few of those campaigns showed any evidence of being structured to take those audiences from that engagement towards a sale. At best, brands such as Nike and John Lewis simply used the opportunity to promote their World Cup offers at the audience – i.e. there was no sense of journey for all those who were not immediately interested in making a purchase.

As you start to design your stories, it is a useful exercise to firstly see how many 'threshold crossings' you can list. You can narrow this down to a list that you think will be most successful – you have to get creative! This is where you review the attitude heat maps, which of these can you use when they are positive and which do you need to change? Crossing the threshold should address or use these.

You must also appreciate that the content pillar does not end when you have crossed the first threshold. It must continue through all the stages or you will create a disconnection in the experience that they have with you. Having purchased, the relationship between the customer and the brand should not simply revert to, for example, billing and customer service. If you do that then you have lost the essence of what drew the audience to you in Act 1 which in turn prompted the purchase. Instead, you must continue to base the relationship around the content pillar. So if the content pillar is 'property investment' then engagement around property investment should continue through Act 3 and take advantage of the new channels that may now be open to you as a brand in communicating with your customer.

This is what we mean with regards to our example:

Mutuality/ Pillar	Ordinary World	Threshold
Property: *Extending & Renovating*	So many things to remember when doing a home DIY project. • How to manage time. • How to make sure everything is done properly. • How to budget for the change. • How to fund it all.	Whilst considering all the things to do, how will I fund this project? I can't afford it out of savings, therefore I should just not do the project. Reveal the possibilities of re-mortgaging and how easy that is to do.
Property: *Moving home.*	We really need some extra space as the family is growing, but can't extend the house. Moving home is so difficult and expensive. We could get stuck in a chain. We don't know what all the costs of moving house will be.	Here's a list of all the things you need to remember when moving house and here are some hints and tips about keeping the costs down. By the way, we can wrap some of these costs into your new mortgage and help you in other ways with your move, such as the insurance costs.

Engagement Maps

This first table shows you what to write into each column with an example from the first scene. We will then show you through the subsequent tables the rest of the journey, but without these hints. So, start by defining all the content and then move on to complete all the other information. It is important to break up the work by thinking about the content independently from how you are going to deliver it.

Content Pillar: Moving Home		Act 1: Ordinary World	
Map & track entry content	CONTENT	Audience journey	Beginning to think about moving, the house just isn't big enough for us.
		Content goal: enter	Capture audience as the hub for all information about moving home.
Map & track engagement content		Content goal: engagement	Moving home is hard, one of the 4 most stressful things that happen in life. Engage around all the challenges and where to get started.
Map & track exit content		Content goal: exit	This is the place to find all I need to know about moving home.
Specify which personas are relevant to each content focus	PERSONAS	Persona tags	Dinkys
Identify where content engagement will be delivered – e.g. hub, third party publisher, etc.	CHANNEL	Primary channels	New property website.
Ensure channels & content vehicles exist for content goal		Channel audit	Need a new site, won't work in our current sites.
Specify channels that will support content journey		Secondary triggered channels	E-mail, social.
Specify campaigns that will support content journey		Campaign triggers	E-mail to let them know about our new content.
Specify priority of content stage	METRICS	Priority	Top priority to build the audience.
Analytics of audience progression by content consumption		Audience analytics	Count site hits and e-mail opens.
Track investment required – e.g. incentives, promotions, rewards		Budget	£10,000.

Nurture

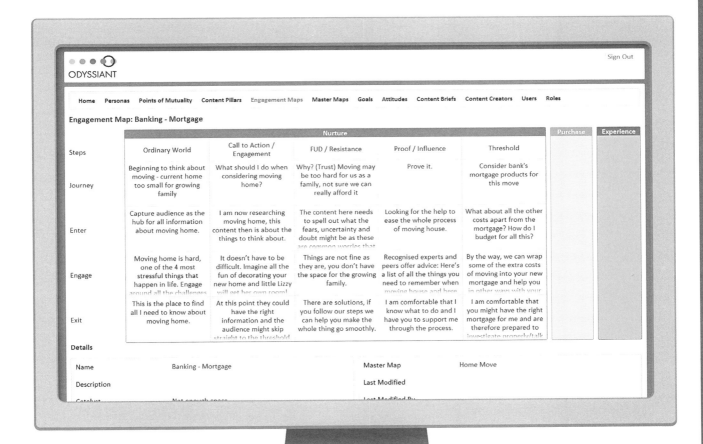

Sign Out

ODYSSIANT

Home   Personas   Points of Mutuality   Content Pillars   Engagement Maps   Master Maps   Goals   Attitudes   Content Briefs   Content Creators   Users   Roles

Engagement Map: Banking - Mortgage

	Nurture					Purchase	Experience
Steps	Ordinary World	Call to Action / Engagement	FUD / Resistance	Proof / Influence	Threshold		
Journey	Beginning to think about moving - current home too small for growing family	What should I do when considering moving home?	Why? (Trust) Moving may be too hard for us as a family, not sure we can really afford it	Prove it.	Consider bank's mortgage products for this move		
Enter	Capture audience as the hub for all information about moving home.	I am now researching moving home, this content then is about the things to think about.	The content here needs to spell out what the fears, uncertainty and doubt might be as these are common worries that	Looking for the help to ease the whole process of moving house.	What about all the other costs apart from the mortgage? How do I budget for all this?		
Engage	Moving home is hard, one of the 4 most stressful things that happen in life. Engage around all the challenges	It doesn't have to be difficult. Imagine all the fun of decorating your new home and little Lizzy will get her own room!	Things are not fine as they are, you don't have the space for the growing family.	Recognised experts and peers offer advice: Here's a list of all the things you need to remember when moving house and here	By the way, we can wrap some of the extra costs of moving into your new mortgage and help you in other ways with your		
Exit	This is the place to find all I need to know about moving home.	At this point they could have the right information and the audience might skip straight to the threshold	There are solutions, if you follow our steps we can help you make the whole thing go smoothly.	I am comfortable that I know what to do and I have you to support me through the process.	I am comfortable that you might have the right mortgage for me and are therefore prepared to investigate properly/talk		

Details

Name	Banking - Mortgage	Master Map	Home Move
Description		Last Modified	
Catalyst	Not enough space	Last Modified By	

Purchase

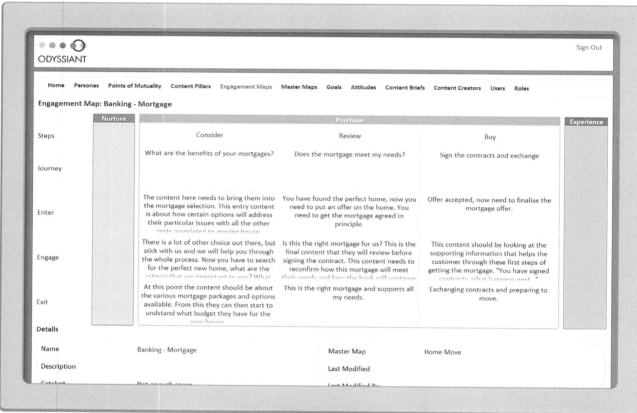

ODYSSIANT

Sign Out

Home   Personas   Points of Mutuality   Content Pillars   Engagement Maps   Master Maps   Goals   Attitudes   Content Briefs   Content Creators   Users   Roles

Engagement Map: Banking - Mortgage

	Nurture	Purchase			Experience
Steps		Consider	Review	Buy	
		What are the benefits of your mortgages?	Does the mortgage meet my needs?	Sign the contracts and exchange	
Journey					
Enter		The content here needs to bring them into the mortgage selection. This entry content is about how certain options will address their particular issues with all the other costs associated to moving house	You have found the perfect home, now you need to put an offer on the home. You need to get the mortgage agreed in principle.	Offer accepted, now need to finalise the mortgage offer.	
Engage		There is a lot of other choice out there, but stick with us and we will help you through the whole process. Now you have to search for the perfect new home, what are the criteria that are important to you? What	Is this the right mortgage for us? This is the final content that they will review before signing the contract. This content needs to reconfirm how this mortgage will meet their needs and how the bank will continue	This content should be looking at the supporting information that helps the customer through these first steps of getting the mortgage. "You have signed contracts, what happens next..."	
Exit		At this point the content should be about the various mortgage packages and options available. From this they can then start to undstand what budget they have for the new house	This is the right mortgage and supports all my needs.	Exchanging contracts and preparing to move.	

Details

Name	Banking - Mortgage	**Master Map**	Home Move
Description		**Last Modified**	
Catalyst	Not enough space	Last Modified By	

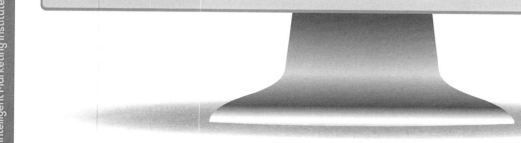

Experience

ACT 3

ODYSSIANT

Sign Out

Home   Personas   Points of Mutuality   Content Pillars   Engagement Maps   Master Maps   Goals   Attitudes   Content Briefs   Content Creators   Users   Roles

Engagement Map: Banking - Mortgage

	Nurture	Purchase	Experience			
			Receive	**Experience**	**Acknowledge**	**Advocate**
Steps			Mortgage money goes to the seller and we get some to help with the moving costs	That was easy, we've got the money	We've moved in!	The bank were so helpful every step of the way
Journey						
Enter			Confirmation that everything has gone through.	A to-do list of things to sort out for moving day. Think about a budget for all the additional costs you might have for the move	Welcome to your new home.	You've got the new home, now you need to make it yours.
Engage			You've got the money, you now need to start planning for moving day.	Moving day. List in hand, make sure the dog and cat are in kennels so they don't get stressed out!	We are here, settling into our new home. Things that you now need to do in the new home, for example get your utilities sorted out and pick your	The redecorating begins!
Exit			So many things to plan and think about where to begin?	Everything has gone smoothly.	Make sure you have your home set up to be efficient.	Start on a new content pillar/journey.

Details

Name	Banking - Mortgage	Master Map	Home Move
Description		Last Modified	
Catalyst	Not enough space	Last Modified By	

Plan

Now that the engagement maps have been defined, we can create the first draft of the plan. This will be the first draft as it will evolve and continue to develop as you learn through measurement what does and does not work.

The plan covers two areas:

1. **Editorial calendar:** This is the production plan for the content.

2. **Campaign 'lay-down' plan:** The lay-down plan covers what campaigns you are going to run and when. Whilst this plan will start to shift as you embed your audience engagement strategy, you will still be doing some communications that you are already doing regularly. For example, you may have seasonal or legislation notices that you send out at certain times of the year.

Our plan needs to cover both these areas so that you can make the change to the audience engagement strategy without disrupting your normal communications or causing a problem with your customers. The contact strategy (if you are skim reading then note we used the word 'contact' not 'content'!) will be written separately to make sure that we do not over communicate with our audience, it will be referenced by the content Decision Engine when executing the plan – more on the contact strategy in a moment.

Month	Persona	Pillar	Act/ Scene	Campaign Sustain	Channel	Foundation	Content Title	Call to Action/ Goal	Due Date
1	Dinkys	Moving Home	1, Ordinary World	Sustain	Microsite	Entertain, educate.	The trials of moving home.	Go to microsite on moving home.	Mid-month
1	Dinkys	Moving Home	1, Ordinary World	Sustain	Microsite	Entertain, educate.	Tips and tricks for managing the stress of moving house.	Go to microsite forum with all the tips for moving home.	...
1	Dinkys	Moving Home	1, Ordinary World	Sustain	Microsite	Entertain, educate.	Checklist, what to remember when moving home.	Go to check-list page and engage on the forum with questions.	
1	Dinkys	Moving Home	1, Call to Adventure	Campaign	E-mail	Educate, convince.	Climbing the property ladder made easy.	Go to the microsite.	
1	Dinkys	Moving Home	1, Refusal of the Call	Campaign	E-mail	Convince, inspire.	The status quo won't be that way for long.	Go to the microsite.	
April	All	N/A	N/A	Promotion	Letter	Education	ISA – savings plans	Go to website.	April 1st.

The Brief

Now that you have created the maps and your plan of what you want to do, the next step in execution is to brief people as to what needs to be done. What changes here significantly over what you have done in the past is the nature of the brief that you now give to your writers/creators for each item. This is where you now need to take on the role of editor-in-chief. To meet your publishing timescales you have to work like a publishing house and set strict deadlines and quality criteria.

However, now you have a lot of detail in your audience engagement strategy you can use

this to create much more detailed briefs – you can also look at curating your content; if you have created the POM properly this should be much easier to do than if you were trying to curate for your own brand or product.

From the engagement map above we can then select the cell that we want to create a content brief for:

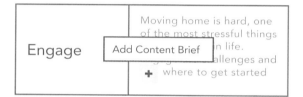

Example brief:

Audience:	Dinkys
POM:	Property
Pillar:	Moving Home
Act/Scene:	Act 1, Ordinary World
Campaign/Sustain:	Sustain
Channel:	Microsite
Due Date:	Mid-month
Content Brief:	Moving home is hard, one of the 4 most stressful things that happen in life. Engage around all the challenges and where to get started.
Goal for this piece of content:	Engagement
Call to action:	Click to next article in series.
Scope:	1000 words, article style.

Contact Strategy

The contact strategy contains the rules that help us make sure that we are not over contacting our audience. It is often difficult to get the contact strategy put in place as it usually means that product managers have fewer customers to talk to. This is where the audience strategist role needs to have some teeth. It must not be possible for a product manager to override the contact or audience engagement strategy or you will harm the relationships with your customers and damage the plan. More importantly, you will not make as much money!

The contact strategy will usually vary by channel of communication and product or service and it usually only applies to outbound communication; after all, the customer can contact you whenever they like!

As an example, you might have a rule that says it must be six weeks between calls for our insurance products in our bank. We might also say that phone calls should always be on a Wednesday evening between 7 p.m. and 8.30 p.m. Part of this is insight, part of it is courtesy. Our insight tells us which day of the week and time of the day people are more receptive to offers, but we also have to recognise that we are interrupting their day, so if you call earlier they may be having an evening meal or travelling home from work. The contact strategy stops you from over contacting your audience. But, as we have shown above, if you create the right story that your audience wants to engage with, this will become less important.

SUMMARY

What you will have achieved by this stage is a complete strategy for how to engage with your audience in a new way. You will also have converted your strategy into a delivery plan so that you can start briefing your delivery teams. Very soon you will be publishing your new content.

In this chapter

- Engagement Decision Engine Functions
- Integration to Engagement Strategy Planner

Engagement Decision Engine

The next item, as we work our way down through the ICE architecture, is the Engagement Decision Engine. This component sits in the 'future capability' box. The Engagement Decision Engine will become a vital capability if you have millions of customers and lots of communications that you need to orchestrate. It is worth noting that the Engagement Decision Engine is now a possibility because of advancements in various technologies. Whilst these technologies exist, it is not yet fully available in the manner needed to integrate to the Engagement Strategy Planner as we describe below in order to be driven by our audience engagement strategy.

Manual Workaround

The manual workaround for this is to directly push your briefs into your delivery capabilities. It means that you will not be able to monitor your audience journeys automatically and you will need to do this by tracking campaigns and web traffic. However, you will have changed what you are publishing so you will have started the process of changing how your audience engages with you and, more importantly, you will be deliberately creating content that will enable your audience to cross the threshold.

The following diagram shows you where it sits in our overall architecture:

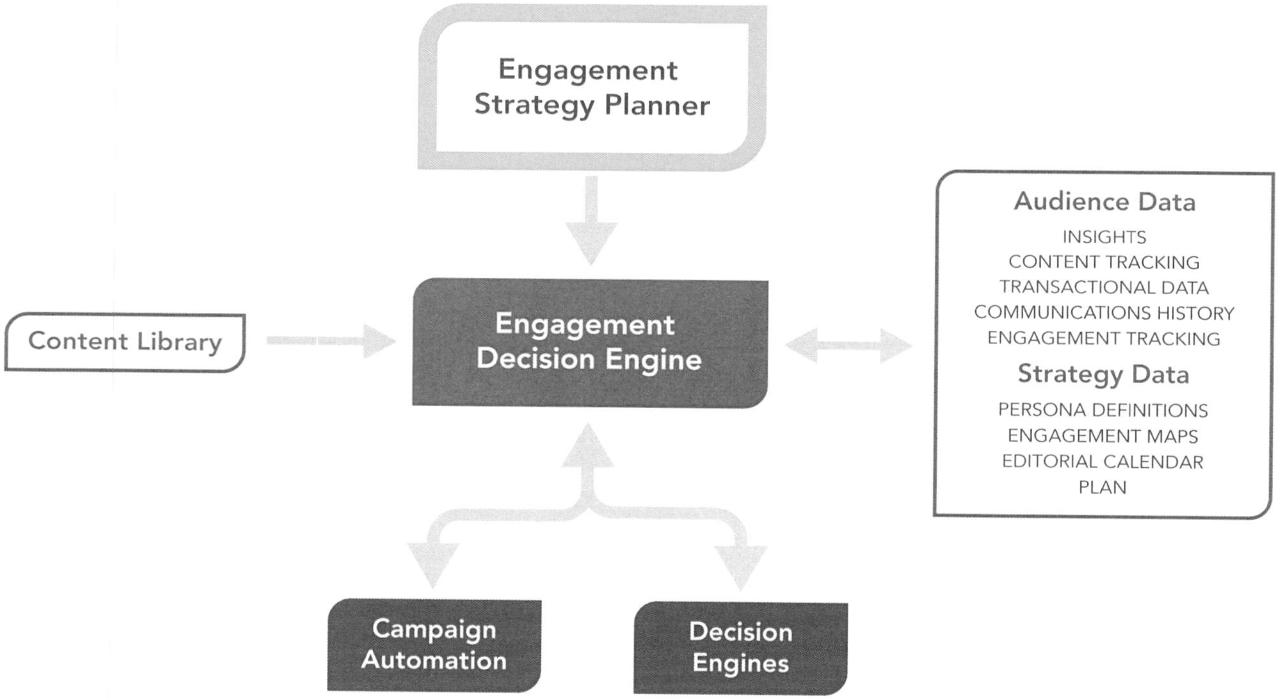

Engagement Strategy Planner

Content Library

Engagement Decision Engine

Campaign Automation

Decision Engines

Audience Data

INSIGHTS
CONTENT TRACKING
TRANSACTIONAL DATA
COMMUNICATIONS HISTORY
ENGAGEMENT TRACKING

Strategy Data

PERSONA DEFINITIONS
ENGAGEMENT MAPS
EDITORIAL CALENDAR
PLAN

The Intelligent Marketing Institute

The Engagement Decision Engine will perform a number of tasks that we have broken down into steps below:

STEP

1

Consume & Understand Content

The ability to consume content into a database and then understand the meaning of it is now possible with NLP (Natural Language Processing) technology. The result of consuming the content and then running this process is that each item is then 'tagged' with topics that are the key topics for the item. A 'topography' is used to understand the links between items. For example the phrase 'The jaguar purred as it ate the antelope', means that the jaguar is a cat and not a make of car. The topography understands brand and product names and that the name of a famous person is just that – a person. It is these tags that we can use to both define what should be in our content and which piece of content then is appropriate for a particular part of our journey.

For example, for our bank:	
Content Pillar:	Moving Home
Act 1, Scene 1:	Ordinary World
Tags:	Moving Home, Moving Stress, Cost of Moving, Finding the Right Home, Mortgages, Mortgage Calculator – there may be many more.

Publish

STEP

2

If you have followed the process so far, you will have created your audience engagement maps and then pushed these into the editorial calendar and the laydown plan. Your content production team will have responded to the content brief and you now have some content to deliver.

The Engagement Decision Engine will (in future) be used as your delivery mechanism for the content. It will decide what content to deliver to whom and through what channel by taking instructions from the ESP. It will also determine what channels each piece of content is delivered through. The Engagement Decision Engine will provide the automation of delivering the content to the audience.

Remember, you do not have to create everything that you publish, you can curate content and then republish it. However, at the moment you can only track the content that you publish within your own digital assets; it is not possible at the time of writing to track your audience when they are not on your web properties.

Track the Consumption of the Content

STEP

3

When your audience turns up and consumes your content within your own digital assets, you can then track this at an individual level. Tracking can be anonymous or, if they have logged into an account of some sort, it can be tagged to an identified person. What is important here is that you are able to track how effective each item of content is by looking at dwell time and where your audience clicks on to. The methods for doing this are constantly evolving, particularly as the laws around cookies continue to change.

4

Build Persona Interest Clouds

Your audience does not just consume the content and then move on. Remember the 'tags' in step 1? These now get associated to the consumer as they move from content item to content item. This creates individual and persona interest clouds. If I visit a topic only once, then my interest in that topic is degraded over time. Conversely, if I keep going back to the same topic then my interest level increases. I do not just get the main topic, I will get all the topography associated with that. For example, if I read an article on David Beckham it will also associate Football, Manchester United, Victoria Beckham, and so on. If I then moved on from David to Victoria I would get Fashion, Spice Girls and Music. My interest level in Football would then go down.

The Engagement Decision Engine can then 'aggregate' these individual interest clouds to a persona level. This insight about real (and current) interests of personas can then feed back into the persona definitions. Once new persona definitions are available it also means that the POMs, pillars and audience engagement maps can change to reflect this new insight and optimise the audience engagement strategy.

STEP

5

Start 'Pushing' the Journeys

When an invidual is consuming our content, the Engagement Decision Engine will be able to check where they are on the journey and what should be served next to move them along. It should also refer to their interest cloud and serve something that is relevant and interesting to the individual. It should deliver the next relevant piece (or pieces) of content no matter what channel the individual is in. In this way the individual can join any story at any point and always get what comes next logically and is of interest to them. By monitoring this we will be able to see people get 'stuck' at certain points in our story and then use a campaign to nudge them forward.

SUMMARY

Engagement Decision Engines are not yet delivering on the functionality we described but this will be coming soon. By setting up your audience engagement maps manually you will be ready for this advancement. Whilst you will not be learning in an automated way, by tracking content consumption – from open rate in e-mail, for example – you will be learning what content works to move your audience towards a sale.

In this chapter

- Decision Engines' Functionality
- Integration to Engagement Strategy Planner

Decision Engines

The next items on the ICE architecture that we need to take a look at are the campaign automation tools and Decision Engines. Both these capabilities can be performed by existing technologies available from a number of different vendors. However, we will be describing Decision Engines in a good degree of detail because as a capability they are generally less well understood.

A Decision Engine is most commonly used within 'inbound' channels to make sure that the business is taking the right action with each person. This is important within our ICE architecture as a Decision Engine is one of the capabilities that we will use to execute our audience engagement strategy.

However, to start with the obvious, what is a Decision Engine and how does it work? In the reference chapter within the appendix we cover how statistical models are built; if you do not understand statistical models we suggest you have a quick read of that chapter. This is because Decision Engines harness the power of statistical models by combining them with rules in order to prompt an action. However, there are many ways in which this can be achieved and there are a number of products on the market that say they are making decisions, but they are not necessarily a Decision Engine.

What They Do…

Let's start with a simple selling decision: which product should we offer a customer when they contact us with a service query? It is worth remembering that Decision Engines started life in contact centres but are now more widely used in digital channels. As such, our example will be a decision that is made in the contact centre as each customer calls in. This means that we will have some context of the customer's situation before we make the decision.

The following diagram represents the components we need to make the decision of what to offer the customer:

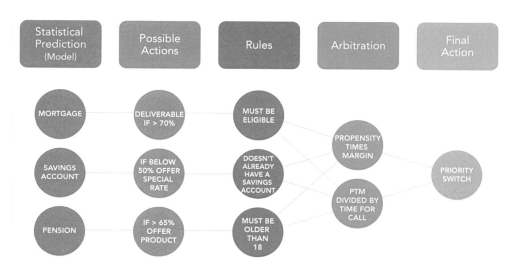

Building the decision starts from the left with the predictive models (grey balls). Sticking with our banking example, we have three models that will predict the customer's likelihood to purchase three different products. In reality, decisions are a lot more complicated than shown above as there may be many more models and rules that are used in each set. However, they can be built up like this, one product, service or decision at a time.

For each model we then need to define the actions that can be taken (blue balls). In the example we have just shown one action for each, but more normally there would be three or four actions and this is a way of segmenting the model; 'segmenting' the model is usually done by high, medium and low propensity. You can then have different treatments for each segment. For example, if your propensity is low (perhaps only 20% likely to say yes) for a purchase action we may need to give you an extra incentive to buy, such as a discount. You can create as many segments within the model as you like but it will make the Decision Engine run slower and will not necessarily improve your outcomes because more often than not you cannot make that much difference in the treatments. For this banking example, we will only offer a deal if the likelihood to accept is over 70% or in the high segment. Therefore, this means our model would only have two segments: high and low.

For each product, there will be rules as to whether or not you can buy the product. The pink balls are where we add these rules. You may wonder why you would not start with these rules. The answer is that while we are building the decision left to right, it will 'fire' right to left – 'fire' means when the code is actually executed. It runs 'backwards' for efficiency reasons; you do not want to run all the models for every decision as this takes a lot of processing power. So, we will check if the target customer is eligible for the product before we go any further and run any models to sell the product to them. For the specific example for our bank we should run a credit check model before we offer them a mortgage, as we do not want them to fail the credit check after we have tried to sell it to them.

What 'fired' means for our contact centre example is that the software that a contact centre agent is using to manage the call with the customer will send the customer data to the engine and ask it for a decision. The returned decision is then displayed to the agent for them to use in the conversation. It is worth noting that many of the Decision Engine tools have an application 'front' that will allow the display of the decisions and capture of the responses. In digital channels the front-end application is usually embedded into websites.

Next we need to arbitrate between the products. Arbitration is about how you decide what to offer to the customer if they have a good propensity for more than one action. If this was a campaign it is likely that the contact strategy would dictate how often each product manager gets to communicate to the customer – or the product managers may just have a bun fight! However, as this is all happening in real-time we need to set some rules in the decision so it can choose which option to go for as we cannot consult with the product managers every time. In our example we have put in two arbitration rules. The first one simply selects the product that has the greatest sum of the propensity times the margin (the profitability of the product). The second rule also then divides this by the amount of time it takes to sell the product – this assumes that all these products can be sold over the phone, which may not be possible in reality.

The last 'priority switch' will then monitor the call queue lengths in the contact centre and determine which of the arbitration rules wins. If it is a busy time, then products that are quicker to sell would be selected.

Whilst this is the reality of many decisions that are operating in contact centres, it is not actually very customer-centric. If you are new to this, you may be thinking that this is the most customer-centric approach that you have seen for selling to customers. However, a note on arbitration. We have found through extensive research in a number of projects that if you take out the margin rules, longer term you make more money.

To explain, consider the following:

	Product A	Product B
Propensity	55%	85%
Margin	£100	£50

With a margin rule in place, the customer would be offered product A. However, they are more likely to say 'no' to that option. Without the margin rule in place they would be offered product B and they are more likely to say 'yes'. This is more customer-centric as you are offering the customer what they are more likely to want. However, you may be surprised to learn that you will make more money this way. This is because firstly, you have more accepted offers overall. Secondly, our research has shown that the first 'yes' will increase the propensity for the customer to purchase on the second product. In other words, one 'yes' leads to another. The first product sale creates more 'engagement', which makes it easier to sell the second product.

A real-time Decision Engine will make multiple decisions in each interaction. Let's take our banking example: a customer phones in to the contact centre with a request for a quote on household buildings insurance. Given that is what they have asked for, the propensity to buy that product will be pretty high. We deal with their request and they purchase the buildings insurance. Now the Decision Engine runs again and this time the household contents insurance will come up as a high propensity to purchase by that customer. We make this offer, but they say no to that. The Decision Engine runs again and suggests a credit card. This sequence is just an example, the offers will come in the order that is determined by the model scores and rules in the Decision Engine. After each response from the customer the decisions are fired again and we are always presented with the next-best thing to say for the customer that we are dealing with. The only limit to the number of offers or actions within an interaction is how many there are defined within the Decision Engine.

Our decision so far, though, has only considered three product sales. There are, of course, many more products and other decisions that need to be added and they can be built up as components as follows:

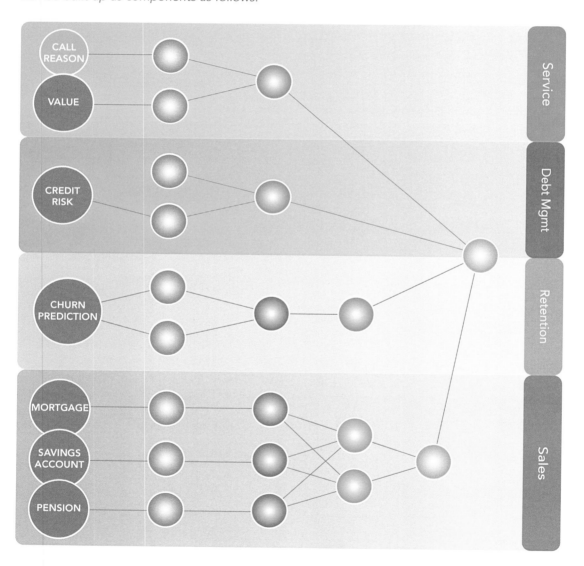

The point to note is that with a real-time Decision Engine, there is no predetermined action. In other words, the models and the decision structure is **only** fired in real-time when the customer turns up and their context is known. As a consequence, through the stages of the conversation the models are scored and information from the last part of the conversation is added to the decision if it is a data item within one of the models, thus changing the score for the next decision.

Integrating Decisioning Into ICE

With the description above you are now up to speed with what has been deployed in more advanced organisations on our maturity model (see section 2, chapter 3). Implementing a Decision Engine would take them to level 4. The next step to implementing the ICE architecture is to now integrate the ESP to the Decision Engine. We discussed previously that it is a very tricky job to integrate decisioning with campaign management but we can do it through the Engagement Strategy Planner.

In the example above, when our customer called into the contact centre they made a specific request that gave the Decision Engine a start point or context of the customer's call. In the ICE world, once we have identified who the customer is the Decision Engine can 'get' the context from the Engagement Decision Engine. This assumes that we have been engaging with the customer through content; if this is not the case then the Decision Engine will take its start point as it normally would. The Engagement Decision Engine can supply the context as it will track individuals within the journey maps that we have defined. It will know the last piece of content that they consumed and therefore which journey they are on and how far along they are. The Decision Engine can then use this as a prediction of what the customer is most likely calling about. That is the first part of the integration.

In the second part of the integration, when the Decision Engine is proposing what action should be taken it can 'get' content that would support that decision. It will therefore be driven by the ESP as to which piece of content should be served to this customer next. When the Decision Engine records the outcome of the decision this is also fed back to the ESP to be used to determine if the customer has moved along the journey. Normally the Decision Engine is at the point of the sale in the customer's journey, therefore we can use this integration to test that our engagement map is doing the job of getting people to this point.

The following diagram shows the connections between the components:

Engagement Strategy Planner

| PLAN | < | Engagement Maps |

↕

Engagement Decision Engine

↕

Decision Engines

SUMMARY

A Decision Engine can make a big difference to the experiences that your customers receive, but it generally will not stretch to engagement before the sale has happened and therefore audience engagement. Having mapped your audience engagement strategy you will be able to enhance the post sales experiences with content through the Decision Engine and make sure that these experiences are in line with the journey that the customer has been on with you so far.

Technology Notes

Not all software products are doing decisioning as we have described above, although they may make the claim that they are a real-time Decision Engine. We have created the following spectrum of complexity to clarify what the different tools do and hopefully help you navigate this area when you are making your own selection. You do not necessarily need a real-time Decision Engine; good results can be achieved all the way along this spectrum and you will need to consider your business requirements to determine what is most appropriate.

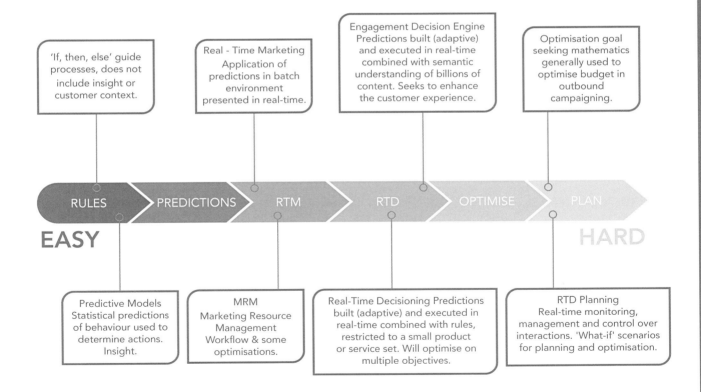

'If, then, else' guide processes, does not include insight or customer context.

Real - Time Marketing Application of predictions in batch environment presented in real-time.

Engagement Decision Engine Predictions built (adaptive) and executed in real-time combined with semantic understanding of billions of content. Seeks to enhance the customer experience.

Optimisation goal seeking mathematics generally used to optimise budget in outbound campaigning.

RULES | PREDICTIONS | RTM | RTD | OPTIMISE | PLAN

EASY

HARD

Predictive Models Statistical predictions of behaviour used to determine actions. Insight.

MRM Marketing Resource Management Workflow & some optimisations.

Real-Time Decisioning Predictions built (adaptive) and executed in real-time combined with rules, restricted to a small product or service set. Will optimise on multiple objectives.

RTD Planning Real-time monitoring, management and control over interactions. 'What-if' scenarios for planning and optimisation.

Quick Summaries:

Rules

Rules are generally 'If, then, else' test type statements that will guide a process. The tests are generally against statistic attributes or can be responses to questions. There is no insight and therefore little flexibility in managing a conversation. Useful for processes where the outcomes are of a fixed nature.

Predictions

Statistical predictive models are built by looking at trends in data to find patterns. The model is then a mathematical formula that customer data can be applied to in order to give a score or a prediction of how likely a customer will exhibit a behaviour. The models can be applied to targeting; for example, within campaign selections. Campaign tools can generally only use one model for a particular selection. Predictions are used by both real-time marketing and real-time decisioning in different ways.

Real-Time Marketing

Real-time marketing applies models to create a campaign that is not executed outbound, it sits and 'waits' for the customer to turn up and then the offer is presented to the customer on the inbound. It is not context-sensitive, meaning that it is not optimised to what the customer just said or did. It is broadcasting on a one-to-one basis! The real-time part is that it is presented in real-time, but there is no processing done in real-time. It should be noted that this will produce reasonable results for a lot of organisations.

Marketing Resource Management (MRM)

MRM tools allow you to plan and budget for marketing activities and programmes; strategic planning and financial management. They allow you to create and develop marketing programmes and content, but are focused on the planning and project management effort. They don't help you determine whether you have created the right plan to meet your engagement objectives. They can also collect and manage content and knowledge (digital asset, content and knowledge management), fulfil and distribute marketing assets, content and collateral (marketing fulfilment) and finally, measure, analyse and optimise marketing resources (MRM analytics).

Real-Time Decisions

We have described real-time decisioning above. The important difference to the other tools and methods is that models are scored in real-time when the customer interacts (any channel). Multiple models can be 'fired' and matrixed together with business rules in order to be reactive to the customer's responses. Because of this a bi-directional negotiation is possible allowing for bundling and deals to occur that are specific to the customer.

Engagement Decisioning

These tools are in the early stages of development, but the requirement is becoming more clarified. Taking our example of the bank's engagement map, this tool would be able to detect where on the journey the individual is and be able to serve the next piece of content that is relevant to that person. This should be integrated with other delivery capabilities; for example, a decision or a campaign may have a specific piece of content that should be delivered with the decision or within the campaign. The engagement decisioning then becomes the mechanism to make sure the audience is progressing along the defined journey and should also be able to measure that, as we shall discuss in the business outcomes section.

Optimisation

Optimisation is generally applied on top of campaign management tools and allows the campaign manager to optimise which campaigns a customer would receive based on the optimisation that they specify. This could be the budget that they have, response rate or revenue, for example. The mathematics used for this type of work is goal seeking. For example, you may want to run 100 campaigns in a month, but you want to optimise who receives which campaign based on a particular goal.

Real-Time Decisioning Planning

These are tools that provide support for management to better optimise the decision rule sets. They allow for different scenarios to be tested by replaying a set of decisions from the past against different thresholds and with different parameters. This way the optimum 'levels' can be set for future decisions.

In this chapter

- Campaign Automation Functionality
- Integration to Engagement Strategy Planner

Campaign Management

The next item on the ICE architecture that we need to take a look at is campaign automation. This is also a capability that can be performed by existing technologies and by a number of different vendors. However, it is important within our ICE architecture as campaign automation is one of the capabilities that we will use to execute our audience engagement strategy.

Engagement
Strategy Planner

Audience Data

INSIGHTS
CONTENT TRACKING
TRANSACTIONAL DATA
COMMUNICATIONS HISTORY
ENGAGEMENT TRACKING

Strategy Data

PERSONA DEFINITIONS
ENGAGEMENT MAPS
EDITORIAL CALENDAR
PLAN

Content Library

Engagement
Decision Engine

Campaign
Automation

Decision
Engines

A campaign is a unit of tasks in marketing and is the equivalent of a project or programme. The reason we suggest this definition for a campaign is because the items that make up a campaign are changing and growing daily, creating an array of different campaign types. The challenge with this is that they operate in silos and independently from each other, which in turn leads to inconsistencies in the messages that your customers receive. In order to achieve maturity in the consistency and unification principle of our maturity model, you need to deliver all these different campaigns within an overarching audience engagement strategy.

All campaigns have a common goal: i.e. to attract customers to your product or service. Where this then starts to become science over art is when you start to optimise where you spend your marketing budget. For example, you do not want to waste your time and money talking to people who are never going to become a customer. At the same time you need to carefully make your product appealing to those that are likely to buy.

Campaign management tools enable companies to define, orchestrate and communicate offers to customer segments across multichannel environments, such as websites, mobile, social, direct mail, call centres and e-mail. This approach can include integrating marketing offers with sales for execution. Basic campaign management includes functionality for segmentation, campaign execution and campaign workflows. Advanced analytic functionality includes predictive analytics and campaign optimisation. Advanced execution functionality includes loyalty management, content management, event triggering, and real-time marketing/offer management in inbound and outbound environments.

If you are new to this, then this probably seems a little confusing, so in order to clarify it let's start by looking at all the campaign types:

- **Advertising Campaign**
  TV
  Radio
  Media – Papers/Magazines
  On-Line Media – Pay Per Click (PPC)

- **PR Campaign**

- **Database Marketing**
  Direct Mail Campaign
  E-mail Campaign

- **Search Campaign**
- **Social Campaign**
- **In-bound Decisioning**
  (Real-Time Marketing)

The first two main bullet points are usually considered 'above the line' and the rest 'below the line'. What this means is that the items below the line are usually 'addressed' to someone. This is known as your addressable audience. Above the line can be seen by everyone but is also usually targeted at a particular audience in the way that the messages are delivered; because advertising is so visible this is what a lot of people think marketing is purely about – we can thank *Mad Men* for that. However, as digital technologies advance, the 'line' is starting to get blurred and even a television advert can be delivered to a specific audience.

Campaign Automation

For below the line campaigns we use campaign automation tools. If you are not a campaign planner the way most campaign automation tools work is by a 'waterfall' method. What this means is that you start with the data for your whole audience and then you start to split them up into different 'cells'. These cells will then get different communication treatments. It is referred to as a waterfall because as you develop the campaign you will start to exclude recipients, meaning that the cells get smaller and smaller. Once you have developed the cells, then the communication treatment is matched to them. The tool can then execute the campaign through the channels that you have specified.

In order to successfully progress to maturity in ICE we need to start from a 'top-down' approach to our communications. What this means is that we start with an audience engagement strategy (the top) that aligns to the business goals overall and not individual product or service goals that are often just the goals for this quarter or month. Remember, engagement is not about one-off communications that only exist for the life of a campaign. As such, campaigning has to evolve to a continuous model in order to create an ongoing engagement with your audience.

If you are a start-up this is much easier as you do not have vast amounts of legacy to deal with. If you are in a large organisation, the start points will be different in each situation.

Organisational Change

We suggest that you centralise and rigorously coordinate your marketing activities through the ESP so that you create consistent and managed engagement with your audience through all your channels. With a dedicated audience management team acting as the central hub responsible for operational delivery, you can ensure that there is control of all inbound and outbound below-the-line campaign management activity. You should also have a single team maintaining contact rules, acting as the 'gatekeeper' to the customer relationship and deciding which customers should receive specific offers, and when.

Implementing a Decision Engine with campaign management would take you to level 4 on the maturity model. The next step to implementing the ICE architecture is to now integrate the ESP to the campaigns. We discussed previously that it is a very tricky job to integrate decisioning with campaign management but we can do it through the Engagement Strategy Planner.

Integration With ESP

In the case of campaign management, the integration to the ESP is simpler than with a Decision Engine. Campaigns in our new world are executed against the Audience Engagement Plan. What this means is that campaigns are used to start the audience on a journey or to nudge them along if they seem to get 'stuck' and are in one area of the journey longer than they should be. For example, our illustrative bank sends me an e-mail to get me started on the mortgage buying journey. As I am at the beginning it will be some content that is in Act 1, Scene 1 'The Ordinary World'. The campaign planner will select everyone that is not already on a journey and fits the persona profile that we want. The creative designer then receives a brief to produce an e-mail template that will have a 'window' for the content that this person should get. When the campaign is

executed, the campaign management tool will ask the Engagement Decision Engine for the right piece of content to put in this window for this person. The Engagement Decision Engine will check what content should be used for this person that can be put in the e-mail channel. It then matches the two parts together and sends it off. By monitoring the open, click and click-through-rate we can then send back to the engagement planner confirmation that the e-mail was opened and the customer then clicked to a landing site to read some more. Websites can then also track that person when they click through and are served the next part of the story by asking the Engagement Decision Engine for their content.

As the ESP is feeding and monitoring all channels, it provides the integration of a consistent conversation with the audience.

Manual Workaround

MW

As we showed previously, your audience engagement strategy allows you to create much more detailed briefs for your campaigns. In the example above, we leave a 'window' for the Engagement Decision Engine to put the right content in the campaign. In a manual version you will need to specify which content items should go to which audience members and you will personalise it at a cell level rather than an individual level. If you are already running a campaign automation tool then this is not going to change how you do anything currently; you will simply have a more detailed brief as to what content should be delivered. What you will find is that campaigns will evolve to be either 'start' or 'nudge'. What this means is that you will use outbound campaigns to get your audience started on a journey or to move them along if they appear to be stuck. You will also slowly start to move away from campaigns that go straight for the sale – i.e focus purely on Act 2.

SUMMARY

Campaign automation is still an important tool in our new ICE world. How things are done does not need to change at all but what is done will change a lot. It is this change that will cause more organisational change than changing how to do it. Once you have implemented the new briefing process into your campaigning team you will be starting to engage with your audience and taking them on the journeys that you have defined.

In this chapter

- Engagement Strategy Dashboard
- Marketing Resource Management

Engagement Strategy Dashboard

We are now moving back to the top of the ICE architecture diagram as we have started communicating with our audience and we now need to manage and monitor those communications.

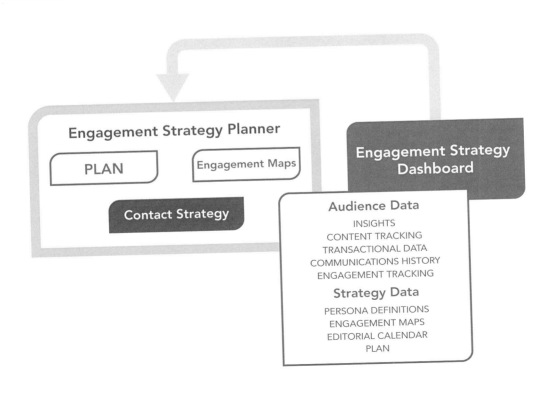

In chapter 2 of this section we described how the ESP would allow you to set up your engagement plan. The Engagement Strategy Dashboard (ESD) is then the tool that we use to assess how well the plan is working.

In the ESD, by using an Engagement Decision Engine we are able to see how many people we have on each journey and what their progress is along that journey.

What this means is that after some time testing and learning about how the journeys are actually travelled by people, we will be able to forecast when and how many goals will be achieved.

Relating to our banking example, our dashboard could look like this:

- 105k people on this journey
- 55k in Act 1
- 31k in Act 2 (30%)
- 19k in Act 3

- 300k people on this journey
- 100k in Act 1
- 159k in Act 2 (53%)
- 41k in Act 3

- 250k people on this journey
- 60k in Act 1
- 177k in Act 2 (71%)
- 13k in Act 3

- 57k people on this journey
- 4k in Act 1
- 51k in Act 2 (91%)
- 2k in Act 3

With the data that we are collecting via the Engagement Decision Engine, there will be many more options of what the dashboards will report on.

The next step from just reporting on the engagement strategy is to be able to try out other ideas. This means that the ESD allows you to test scenarios and 'what-if' cycles where you would re-run part or whole journeys and see if you would get a better result by making some changes. If those changes would be more effective, you would be able to 'commit' those changes to the plan. The next person to come into that part of the journey would then get the new version as served by the Engagement Decision Engine.

Manual Workarounds

There are a couple of options for manual and semi-manual workarounds for the ESD which are as follows:

Reporting/MI

By consolidating the feedback information from campaigns, decisions, websites and any other delivery mechanisms that you are using, you can create a dashboard/report that will consolidate the results of all your activity. You can then use this information to make changes to your audience engagement strategy.

Marketing Resource Management Tools

The second option is to use an MRM tool. 'MRM' stands for Marketing Resource Management. We have said above that this is a semi-automated option because MRM tools are not set up to monitor personas, content pillars and journeys/engagement maps. As such, MRM cannot monitor content the way that we need to in the ICE world. They are, however, very good at managing and monitoring 'old-style' campaigns. In case you are not familiar with MRM, it is a technology for managing your marketing plans and optimising (usually budget driven) all your campaigns. On the face of

it you might think that sounds like the ESP functionality. However, while MRM is about managing a plan, it does not have any checks to say whether you have the right plan and does not help with the actual building of the plan other than by systemising the plan.

At this point the MRM vendors are probably having a fit and contradicting this as they say they will optimise campaigns and report on their effectiveness. However, that does not mean that the overall plan or engagement has been planned as we have described in this book. The optimisation in MRM tools is looking at the effectiveness of individual campaigns, but in our ICE world we are looking to create sustained engagement and therefore the old measures do not work.

However, for clarity this what most MRM tools do:

- Planning – helps to manage the marketing process from strategy development and planning, to creation of marketing assets, to marketing campaign execution, to post-campaign analysis and reporting. ('Helps' means that it provides you with checklists of things you should think about and streamlines your marketing processes. All very useful stuff, but it is not designing the engagement strategy.)

- Financial management – provides visibility into time frames, costs and overruns via dashboards and reporting capabilities.

- Digital asset management – delivers value from existing assets by enabling greater collaboration among marketers with an integrated infrastructure that facilitates the sharing of effective materials and processes, which might otherwise be kept on marketers' PCs or departmental servers.

- Workflow – creative and other approvals processes. This can be very useful if this is normally a bottleneck for you.

- Marketing mix optimisation – affords an easy way of analysing, forecasting and optimising the mix of advertising and promotions.

- Monitoring marketing performance management – determines the right metrics to track as well as identifying the most profitable customers. Helps marketers determine the optimal allocation of marketing resources, whether they relate to direct channel communication or indirect media advertising and promotions.

MRM will work as a semi-manual workaround as it will provide you a consolidated view of the performance of all your communications. The first option is probably cheaper but you may already have an MRM tool implemented. If you do, you will need to repurpose it to manage and run your audience engagement strategy. repurposing it will start by replacing the campaigns currently in your plan with your new ones.

SUMMARY

Once you are able to monitor your activity with real-time feedback loops you will be able to more quickly adapt and refine your audience engagement strategy. Over time you will start to see what works and how quickly it works. Forecasting sales with accuracy will then become a reality for any organisation implementing the ICE methodology.

In this chapter

- Implementation Plan
- Staging
- Managing Change

Implementation Plan

We have now outlined all the components of ICE, and therefore in this chapter we will now look at the stages you need to go through to implement it. There are several journeys that you need to go on as an organisation when implementing ICE and the steps you will need to take will very much depend on the make-up of your organisation – your own internal personas! – and the journeys you will need to take them on. The first thing to do, therefore, is to align your people's thinking and emotions to prepare them for the journey that you are going to take them on. It means that you need to be clear about where you want to end up in order to lead your organisation there. It needs to be an exciting vision to get people on your side and you need to believe passionately about the destination. This is all the normal leadership stuff that you would expect when embarking on a change programme, but do not think you can skimp on this or miss it out for an ICE implementation as you are going to affect many more areas of the business than just marketing. As we discussed at the beginning, you will have (probably many) silos within your organisation. You have to make sure that each area understands how the new world will work as you move towards this goal.

The following diagram shows you a roadmap of the stages to implement ICE. There are three different 'streams' of work: Organisation, Content, and Technical. This is our suggestion for how you think about the work ahead; however, we recognise that you may have more or fewer streams and stages than this depending on your own journey.

The stages can be followed in a linear fashion or you can run some things in parallel; again, it will depend on your journey and how far you want to go with technical integration before you 'go live' and start delivering content to your audience. We suggest that you do not get 'analysis paralysis' and get stuck in the first two stages by trying to design all possible personas and journeys before you start the communications. A way around this is to run through the stages end-to-end for one group of your audience and for one goal as a proof of concept. You can then iron out any wrinkles and bring on board the rest of your audience and more goals as iterations of your engagement strategy.

	STAGE 1	STAGE 2
ORGANISATION	**EDUCATION & DISCOVERY** • Workshops • Stakeholder Maps • Internal Engagement Map • Roll-out Plan	**DESIGN** • Workshops • Insight Validation
CONTENT	• Insight Analysis • Process Analysis • Content Library Index	• Personas • POMs • Content Pillars • Engagement Maps
TECHNICAL	• Impact Assessment • Roll-out Plan • Requirements Definitions	**PLAN** • Validate Requirements • Assess & Acquire Technology Where Required

ICE Implementation

STAGE 3	STAGE 4	STAGE 5	STAGE 6
ALIGN	CREATE	DELIVER	MONITOR, CONTROL, OPTIMISE
• Process Re-engineering • Contact Strategy Across Silos	• Implement Process Changes	• Execute	• Analyse • Test & Learn

• Contact Strategy • Laydown Plan • Decision Strategies • Content Audit	• 'Sustain' Design & Build • Campaign Design • Cross Channel Design	• Run Campaigns • Go Live With Sustain • Content Decision Engine Live	• Monitor Content • Monitor Journeys • Optimise Content & Journeys
PLAN	**PLAN**		
• Integration Design • Integration Build & Test • Reporting Requirements Build	• Integrate ESP to Campaign • Integrate ESP to Decision Engines	• Go Live	• Go Live With Dashboards

Stage 1: Education & Discovery

Where we typically start, and we therefore recommend you do likewise, is by running a series of brainstorming and education workshops that get everyone on the same page and engaged in shaping how the project will progress. It starts with what are our definitions for marketing, content marketing and the audience engagement strategy; we suggest you go through your internal glossary of terms and make sure that you are using your language consistently. Be aware that one hurdle can often be that you have different meanings across your organisation for the same labels.

During these workshops you will start to discover who is communicating to your customers, how, when and with what. This is the start point of auditing your content and building your content library index. This the list of your content that you can then use for the content audit later on. You will then start to see that each area will have its own processes for the management of content so you will need to work out how to align these.

As you work out who should attend these workshops, you will be creating the all-important stakeholder map. What you will quickly see is that you have lots of 'personas' among your stakeholders who will have different needs and start points for your project. Using a spreadsheet, follow the ICE engagement strategy processes that we have described in the previous chapters to determine what you need to do to take your organisation on this journey; who needs what communication (content), when and how will you deliver it? By completing this exercise on your internal team it will give you good practise for developing your external engagement strategy.

In mapping these journeys your goal is organisational change; this is a process of reducing commitment to the way things are, and increasing commitment to the way things will be. The incorporation of new technologies or processes into an enterprise, business unit or department is viewed as a major event by those who are impacted by the new technologies or processes. These people may not realise the need to shift beliefs or behaviours, and often find the challenge of changing very formidable.

As you deliver your workshops, you will start to spot people that you can bring into your 'virtual' team that will help you with the next tasks.

Stage 2: Design

The design stage is about creating your Audience Engagement Stategy for your external audience. If you refer back to section 3, chapter 2 you will see that we have described the steps that you need to go through for this stage and chapter 2 of this section (section 4) gives you the templates and tools to build it. The steps to create the personas, the content pillars and the engagement maps are not going to be linear. This is normal so do not be afraid to go back and revise your content pillars when you work through the engagement maps. You may think of something as a pillar but then discover as you work through it that, for example, it will not take the audience on the right journey for you to achieve your goals. This work will involve lots of brainstorming and workshops to get all your team's ideas together. You need to do this as a team so that everyone has their own stake in making this successful. Once you have this work completed you then have your audience engagement strategy.

Measurement is going to be vital for you to understand later on what is working and what is not. As such, at this stage you need to consider what you are going to report on and what dashboards you will need to determine if you are being successful. We suggest that you work with your IT department to get these requirements fleshed out. The earlier they know what data they need to build these reports and dashboards for you then the better chance you have of getting what you need for the final step.

Stage 3: Align

In the first stage you will have started a content library index. You now need to go further and build a complete view of what content you have. By aligning the existing content library to your engagement map you can determine what gaps you have. This list of gaps can then be planned into an editorial production calendar.

You then need to review the existing communications from a timing perspective. This is where you will incorporate the existing contact strategy and the existing campaign laydown plan (both described in previous chapters). If you have a Decision Engine in place you will also look at how your audience engagement strategy is integrated to that at this stage.

Gap Analysis

We need to borrow from our friends in IT to determine what we need to build, what we can re-use and what we should scrap. When you get through this stage you might feel that you have more of a chasm than a gap! ICE, though, should be an evolution not a revolution. Start small, as we have suggested, and pick one goal and one persona to get you started. This is why we recommend using gap analysis which is a technique used to identify the differences between the current state and the future state. We can use the following table to quantify what the gaps are and what we want to do about it – the examples used are for the bank that we have been building our audience engagement strategy for and are stripped back so that we can keep things simple for the purpose of explanation.

Audience Engagement Strategy	Content Library/ Campaigns	Gap/Action
• Persona: Dinkys • POM: Property • Content Pillar: Moving Home • Act 1, Scene 1 – Ordinary World • Goal: Capture audience as the hub for all information about moving home.	• Nothing pre-existing.	• Need a campaign to start them on the journey and let them know we have a content hub for all things property. • Need a microsite as a hub for this content as the place to send them from the campaign.
• Persona: Dinkys • POM: Property • Content Pillar: Moving Home • Act 3, Scene 1 – Receive • You've got the money, you now need to start planning for moving day.	• Currently send a welcome home letter which is the same for all customers. Has standard boilerplate legal text and some text welcoming them as a customer.	• Need to change the letter for customers on this journey so that it ties in with their journey.

As you can see, as you go through your audience engagement strategy you will then have a list of things to produce or change. For some items, like the first campaign, it will be a new brief. For others it will be about making changes to your existing communications.

After you have completed the gap analysis, the next job is to take the 'action' column and put it into a content production plan (editorial calendar). This will require collaboration with

your production teams and we suggest that you get a good project manager to help you build this plan.

We mentioned before that you may have an existing laydown plan for your campaigns. The laydown plan is about when you are sending what and to who; it is usually done on a quarterly basis. The following example is from a telecommunications company:

TASK NAME	18/09	25/09	OCTOBER					NOVEMBER				DECEMBER			
			02/10	09/10	16/10	23/10	30/10	06/11	13/11	20/11	27/11	04/12	11/12	18/12	25/12
Quarterly Laydown Plan															
Win Back			◆ 05/10												
Loyalty				◆ 07/10											
Text Promotion						◆ 30/10									
Voice Promotion									◆ 14/11						
Data Promotion										◆ 22/11					
Welcome												◆ 02/12			
Health Check												◆ 08/12			
Christmas Promotion														◆ 15/12	
Roaming Promotion															◆ 24/12

What you will notice is that this tends to be product promotional messages and they are timed simply to not overlap with each other and give the campaign team time to deliver each one sequentially. In your new audience-centric view of the world you will want to cancel some of these and start to replace them with the new journey campaigns

that will lead towards these goals. Some you will leave as they are, although you will replace the content that is being delivered by them. In the example above you would replace the promotions campaigns with journey campaigns and you would replace the content in the 'Welcome' and 'Loyalty' campaigns. This example is very small and it is quite common for companies to have hundreds if not thousands of campaigns per quarter. It means the task of realigning the campaigns will be lengthy, which is why we must restate the need to start small and learn how to embed these new processes into your organisation before you start to expand your deployment. As a final note, be careful not to have a new campaign going into delivery before you have built the content! You must align the editorial calendar to the new laydown plan.

Technically, it is within this stage that you are considering how your various systems will be used and integrated to deliver against the audience engagement strategy. For the above steps you will be able to use the various technologies that we have described in the previous chapters. You will need to work with your IT department to determine what gaps you have and what the best options for you are.

Stage 4: Create

The 'create' stage is where we hit the production process for the content and campaigns. As the name suggests it is where the creative teams come into their own. From an organisation perspective, this is where you need to consider your process changes as you move towards having an editorial team. This needs to be a serious consideration as you are likely to need to get a lot of content produced and approved quickly. By having an editor-in-chief you can streamline that approvals process.

Up to this point we have not stated on our plan what channels should be used for the content. We have deliberately parked this until now as there should be some creative licence to determine where best to deploy the content. The content should be omnichannel where possible as, for example, you might use social media to push the audience to your website. This will all be defined in the brief from the audience engagement strategy that will describe the goal for each piece of content or campaign. It is then left to the creative team to determine the best channel or channels to meet that brief.

Alternatively, if you are not comfortable leaving this to the creative team you can add the channel strategy to the engagement plan.

Stage 5: Deliver

At this stage you start publishing. We suggest that you start by creating any microsites or content hubs that you are going to need as this is where you will mostly be doing your sustained engagement. The majority of your Act 1 is likely to be through these sorts of content vehicles and your initial campaigns will be about driving your target audience to these locations so that you can start them on their journeys. This, by default, means we are suggesting that you start in Act 1. Remember it is the audience's journey and not yours, and as such you are building the content to support their journey. By making sure they can cross that first threshold, the content will then also bring them towards considering you and your products.

Stage 6: Monitor, Control, Optimise

You will not get this right first time. You must monitor everything that you can as you need to know how effectively everything is working. This stage is therefore about implementing dashboards and reporting as we have described in the previous chapter. Having said that, whilst we are implementing the dashboards now, you should have defined your reporting much earlier on (Stage 2). If you do not do this in the early stages it becomes an afterthought and you are not going to monitor it properly. Now that you are actually delivering the communications, however, your reporting requirements are going to change. This is because when you reach this stage you will have a clearer picture not only of what it is possible for you to do as an organisation, but also what is technically possible.

SUMMARY

The stages we have outlined will step your organisation through the change to Intelligent Customer Engagement. It will probably be a bumpy road despite our guidance but we hope to have smoothed out some of the bumps for you. As we develop this further we will provide you with more tools that will help you and these will be available from our website – address on the back of the book.

We would love to hear about how you get on and read your case study, so please get in touch with us through our website.

SECTION

5

The Business Outcomes of an Audience Engagement Strategy

Adopting a content-led approach improves the way your business is able to engage and interact with your prospects and customers with the result that you can align your business around the audience journey. It is because of this simple fact that an audience engagement strategy is able to produce better outcomes for your business. However, the way in which business outcomes are measured will change quite significantly.

Understanding why this is the case comes back to the already stated point that an audience engagement strategy is not simply a bolt-on tactic within your marketing programme. Instead it is a complete step change for the way in which you market your business and structure it organisationally, the net result being a range of profound commercial benefits.

Benefits for Your Audience

However, before we dive into the benefits the audience engagement strategy will bring to your business, we should first look at it from the audience's point of view. Not many business initiatives would start by talking about the genuine benefits to the audience, but in this instance it is both right to do so and logical. After all, what you will have achieved is to pivot your organisation from a single-minded focus on promoting products and services for your target audience to buy, to a new culture where you are addressing your audience's needs through the products and services you are able to offer. In other words, the needs of your audience now come first.

Put yourself in your audience's shoes for one moment and think through what the experience will have been like when engaging with a brand that has implemented a mature audience engagement strategy. You have engaged with the brand about something you have found genuinely of interest and of use to yourself. You have continued that engagement, consuming more and more content about things that are helping you – be it in the form of entertainment, knowledge, assistance, and so on. Along the way, the brand has offered you something that is directly relevant to your needs and you have, very happily, taken them up on this offer. Having received the product or service, you as the audience have understood how it has met your needs and the way the brand continues to communicate with you is in direct relation to that original need – you are not simply being treated as a consumer of their product but as an individual whose needs the brand genuinely understands because the brand has been engaging with you about that need all the way through the journey. Are you more likely to be an advocate of that brand, stay loyal and buy more? The simple answer is yes. Why? Because the brand has been genuinely helpful not simply through what it sold but in understanding why you would want to buy that product or service in the first place.

This is why we call this approach 'Intelligent Customer Engagement' – because it is the needs of the customer that have been truly met at all stages of **their** journey. Your brand is being truly audience-centric.

Benefits for the Marketer

So now we come to you as a marketer. Put simply, an audience engagement strategy should replace your current marketing methodology which, for the vast majority, could be simply described as 'campaigning'. However, as has also been pointed out in previous chapters, this is not to say that you will no longer run campaigns. The reason for restating this when considering business outcomes is that the same returns that you would measure within your existing campaign-based marketing programme can be applied to a content marketing-based programme with two important differences. Firstly, the returns are more likely to be consistently better and secondly, they can be considered within a much wider context of sustained results. Let's explore that further by taking a simplistic example.

Your typical response rates on any given campaign, using a variety of different tactics, is currently 2% – we are accepting here that many companies would be thoroughly delighted with such a response rate! Within an audience engagement strategy you may still deploy the same tactics, be they anything from digital/social media advertising, to e-mail marketing and so on. The difference is that these tactics are merely the vehicles for delivering the content, which is designed to not only engage the target persona but also form part of a sustained engagement, with a specific journey being delivered. As such, the response rate will be higher within the tactic and additionally the conversion rate of that target persona group over a sustained period of time will be greater as the engagement will cross over between campaigns and be supported by an ongoing engagement programme.

Of course, the above example is overly simplistic and fails to take into consideration the multitude of business objectives that the marketing and communications teams will face. For example, increasing brand awareness may be a higher business priority or, as is increasingly appreciated by many businesses today, reputation management may take precedence. For both of those examples, a content-led campaign will produce positive business results that either far surpass or are impossible through traditional approaches. This is especially because a content-led approach has far

greater levels of message conveyance due to the fact that you are sustaining the engagement with the target audience over a far longer period of time and through a greater volume of content.

Both building brand awareness and managing or repairing your company's reputation requires a sustained engagement with the audience. Campaigning does not, therefore, meet that long-term requirement and brand-building tactics typically lack any element of engagement. Either way, both fall foul of the 'broadcast' dilemma, in that you are simply pushing messages that are all about you, your products or services at the target audience rather than engaging with them and meeting their own expectations and needs.

However, the joy of an audience engagement strategy is that because it is outwardly focused on taking the target audience on an engaged journey, your marketing programme can meet multiple objectives with any given persona. In other words, if the requirement is to mend misconceptions about your company before building the brand awareness as the route to a sale, then an audience engagement strategy will achieve that through the pre-defined engagement maps.

Crucially, to reiterate another point that has already been stated in the book, this approach also maintains engagement with a far greater percentage of your target audience than those who become your customers. In other words, the 98% who did not historically respond are not simply ignored, despite the fact that they are not progressing towards a sale within that particular campaign. Instead the engagement is maintained, with the audience either staying where they are within the journey or, if they have progressed to Act 2, reverting back to the engagement stage of Act 1. Put simply, our approach means that a prospect who does not become a customer today purposefully remains an engaged potential customer of tomorrow.

Tactical Benefits for the Marketer

At the other end of the business outcome spectrum for the marketer are several essential tactical reasons why all companies will have to adopt even the most rudimentary forms of content marketing. This is due to palpable shifts within digital marketing, caused by both the increasing maturity of social media users and the direction Google is taking around its search algorithms.

If you believe your audience is active within social media and therefore there is merit in your company being active on the relevant social media platforms (as defined by your audience being active on them in a context that is applicable to your brand, product or service) then you are going to need a content strategy. Sadly, few companies understand this. That is why the vast majority of social media brand content is ad hoc broadcast messages about anything and everything that the social media writers can dream of that day, as well as the use of social media channels within specific campaigns which then struggle to continue to engage the audience over time. So, if your social media presence is going to have strategic direction, you will be forced to adopt a content strategy.

As regards Google, it is perfectly clear that content is taking over from keywords. Google has declared war on traditional keyword-based SEO in favour of rich content-based search, be it text, image or video. So to maintain search ranking positions, we are all being forced to adopt a content-led approach whether we like it or not. However, it is becoming quickly apparent that simply creating content for the sake of search rankings leads to a poor visitor experience. So at the very least, your website will have to be based around a content strategy of some form.

More widely, however, brands need to understand the concept of digital journeys. A digital journey is where one piece of marketing collateral leads the target audience to a specific destination and content to continue that campaign. Remarkably, very few marketing campaigns do this. A classic example is the much fêted Jean Claude Van Damme Volvo Trucks video of late 2013. As a viral video, this worked superbly, achieving millions of views worldwide and communicating incredibly effectively a key benefit of a Volvo truck. However, what was surprising was that once this excellent video concluded there was no link or follow-through either physically, in terms of an actual url or communicatively, regards how such a brilliant demonstration of Volvo Trucks' 'dynamic steering' would then lead the target audience onwards once they had self-navigated to the additional collateral on the website.

This is not a criticism of either the agency behind the viral video or the Volvo Trucks marketing department. In fact, they are to be applauded for such a brilliantly conceived stunt. Instead it is a demonstration of how even a rudimentary content marketing strategy builds upon existing campaigning methods and enhances it. A persona-based approach would have delivered a forward-looking audience journey for the various audiences, be they drivers, fleet buyers or simply the impressed masses. This would

have begun with a clear content path for those viewing the video in the form of a digital journey, and then proceeded to sustain that audience interest over time.

It must be stressed that content marketing is largely a digital phenomenon in the sense that is the advent of digital in its current guise that has made modern content marketing possible – i.e. we can now attract, engage and then sustain the conversation with someone through digital channels. We can also move that conversation from medium to medium and channel to channel, sustaining that engagement digitally regardless of where that engagement is digitally taking place. A YouTube video takes an audience to a website, which encourages them to follow us on Twitter, where they are then alerted to the next video or even physical event, and so on.

Big Bad Data

An audience engagement strategy is also the answer to the Big Data question when it comes to customer engagement. In other words, if you want to make use of the myriad of data that you have about your customers, and want to make that customer dataset richer, then an audience engagement strategy will make that happen.

That data is the fuel to your persona-based marketing. It allows you to build content around that data and then feed it out to your target audience in a very structured manner. As the target audience engages with and consumes that content, you then gain some deep insights about your customers that you would simply not glean from a traditional 'broadcast' marketing approach.

For example, if you are a bank targeting small businesses with rich and engaging content, you could learn when the business is thinking about a major expansion effort weeks if not months before they discuss it with the customer relationship manager, simply through the related content they are consuming through you. That sort of data-led insight is invaluable.

Internal Business Transformation

Now we come onto the profound transformational effect Intelligent Customer Engagement will have upon not just the marketing function but the business as a whole. This can be summarised as follows:

Integration

Disjointed, siloed and contradictory customer engagement is rife within the vast majority of companies today. What sounds like a damning indictment of corporate structure is nothing more than an observation on how each function has different objectives to achieve.

> *Unfortunately, as far as the audience is concerned, it is still just one company.*

ICE has the potential to provide that missing integration piece within customer engagement. An embedded audience engagement strategy at the heart of the customer engagement process means that each persona and, where relevant, each individual customer can be managed in a consistent manner. Sales, marketing and customer service will all be singing from the same hymn sheet because it is the content that defines the engagement, not simply outbound campaigns, inbound contact and so on.

Consistency

Such external consistency as described above can be mirrored internally. The audience engagement strategy allows the business to pull in the same direction, especially when perceived externally. Any company milestones and announcements will be fed into the engagement plan, ensuring that any form of customer engagement is managed in relation to the business's own corporate journey. An example might be a price rise not jarring with an existing marketing campaign because the commercial team behind making the price rise decision can easily see how that announcement will sit within the external brand narrative.

Focus

All of which means that the marketing department is transformed as a function because the entire organisation becomes audience focused. In short, the business will have undergone a step change putting the audience journey, through the audience engagement strategy, at the heart of its business philosophy. To achieve growth, expansion, P&L targets, or any other business goal, the business will be able to understand how the target audiences can be influenced over the desired time-period to match that objective. In other words, the business understands that by marketing the idea through the audience engagement strategy, the objective can be more easily realised.

The Commercial Gain

When it comes to commercial gains, there are four potential benefits that your company may experience, depending on the nature of your business. The first is, of course, in relation to sales.

Hard numbers may not yet exist, for all of the reasons already explained about the innovative nature of content marketing in general; however, what is clear is that any goal you assign to the audience journey will be based around the uplift this will bring to your business. All of these will fit within pre-defined metrics. For example, you will already have in place the metrics for measuring reputation, customer satisfaction and so on, and will therefore be able to determine the impact of the audience engagement strategy in relation to those metrics.

When it comes to sales, it is not simply that the volume of sales should increase – that is easy to say, but case studies are needed to prove it – but the fact that conversion will increase due to better targeting. This may not actually lead to a greater volume of sales (although we expect this to be the case) but the fact that greater relevance of the engagement means that your conversion rate is better, with the added benefit that those who do not convert are not lost. Instead the engagement

continues until such a time as they are ready to buy. The added advantage here is that by being more relevant, your own outbound marketing will have annoyed the audience less; if they do not react positively by moving forward in the journey, they can still find the current content they are engaging with right and appropriate. The net result is also a lower cost of acquisition, an often overlooked metric but one which would justify a business case all on its own.

The second commercial benefit is around lifetime engagement with the customer. Note, we have not said 'lifetime value'. This is because we are concentrating more on keeping the customer for longer by having a more relevant engagement between the brand and the customer. If this can be achieved then of course the lifetime value will be greater but the emphasis switches to how to maintain the relevant engagement rather than how to simply calculate the potential value of the customer due to their profile or buying history.

Next comes sector leadership and the associated benefit to brand value. To be a leader you have to act like a leader and an audience engagement strategy epitomises that principle. Therefore, by acting like a leader you will receive the associated brand halo effect. In today's world, where reputation has a tangible dollar value connected to it, goodwill is a measurable commercial benefit. Additionally, when or if your company sustains a hit on its reputation, then having an engaged audience already in place means you are in a far better position to influence their perceptions of the crisis and mitigate the damage.

Finally we are going to throw one last gauntlet down onto the ground – the commercial benefit of being able to forecast audience movement. Through your audience engagement strategy you will be able to track the progress of prospective customers as they move through Act One to the purchasing stage within Act Two. Once in place, you will know how many pieces of content it takes, on average, for each persona to progress and how long it takes them to do so. The result is astounding: you will be able to forecast how many people will cross the threshold and enter the buying cycle, and then know how many of those are likely to convert, based on real audience numbers. You will then know what marketing resource to put where so that you can push the engaged audiences along the journey to meet your goals. Now, can you do that today?

In this chapter

- What Lies Ahead

Change is Coming

When we set out to write this book, our aim was to produce a working manual on how to inject a content-led approach into marketing. We wanted to challenge some lazy thinking about content marketing and produce a practical guide about how to use content in a structured manner to engage audiences, with clear commercial outcomes for your business. Obviously the only people who can judge our success in doing this is you, the reader.

However, one of the things we have been acutely conscious of as we have written this book is that we simply do not have the case studies with the hard numbers to back up a lot of the points we are making. That has made producing a practical guide somewhat challenging, but we have had the benefit of the fact that we are practicing what we preach – everything you have read is being tested in live proofs of concept.

That is the reason that we have written this as a living manual that will be continually updated. As time goes by we will be adding the examples, case studies and hard numbers behind everything we say.

However, we stress one of the main points we have reinforced throughout this book which is that the vast majority of businesses today have some form of content marketing in place whether they call it that or not. It is also widely apparent that businesses are ploughing onwards with content marketing regardless of the evidence required for a business case. To that end, we firmly believe that the guidance we have given is practically useful right now for any business.

What we also believe is that the essence of Intelligent Customer Engagement is the next natural evolutionary step that businesses will take, whether they do so in any consciously planned manner or not. Digital has seen to that. It has changed the way businesses have been forced to engage with customers, it has opened up new avenues for engaging and selling to them, and it has firmly snatched any sense of reputation control away from even the most beloved of brands. But digital is still incredibly young and because of its youth it is beset by trends and fads, but above all it is in a constant turmoil of change.

Your challenge is to cut through the chaff and understand what is the core underlying trend. As we have argued in this book, we believe this to be the shift to true audience-centricity, driven by the fact that you can now engage with an audience throughout their true buying journey. That has only become genuinely possible because of digital.

But who knows what else lies ahead. A lot of what we have scoped in this book relies on automating processes which do not yet exist. Now there's a challenge if ever there was one! However, it also shows that future potential for audience engagement, the benefits this will bring, and the impact on companies both structurally and culturally are virtually unfathomable. Indeed, one of the world's largest mobile phone operators described Intelligent Customer Engagement as not simply the most interesting and innovative thing he had seen in quite some time but also the most culturally challenging.

So it's not for the faint-hearted. However, as we have also made clear, you do not need to play a 'wait and see' game while you watch the brave pioneers rush in where angels fear to tread. Whatever your attitude to risk, there are elements within the audience engagement strategy as we have described it that are immediately and practically applicable for you whatever company you are in. Given the current pace of change that is ingrained within modern life, you will almost certainly find yourself moving towards Intelligent Customer Engagement whether or not you actively choose to do so.

NOTES

APPENDIX

1

Reference: Statistics & Predictive Models

Statistics, Predictive Models, Data Mining and Statistical Insight allow you to execute more 'intelligent' campaigns and marketing communications. Firstly, the model building process will give you insight into your audience's behaviour that will allow you to optimise the communication. Secondly, the models will allow you to find the right message and personalise it for an individual. The models are used in two of the marketing capabilities: Campaign Management and Decision Engines. How each of these works and uses the models is described in section 4.

In the ICE architecture, firstly you use the models to get insight when defining your personas. This includes understanding behaviours so that we can design the right journeys to get the audience engaged. Secondly, we use the models along their journey to predict the next-best-thing that we can say to them (or content that we can serve to them).

Once you have the various audience journeys mapped, you will then go through a number of steps to create the content and start delivering this to your audience. Once they are engaging with your content you can then measure that engagement and use the predictive models to help you deliver the right next message to each individual to move them along their journey. The engagement strategy maps will need to be integrated with the Decision Engine to do this.

Background

The statisticians are probably sitting in a corner somewhere in your business and doing some dark art with the data to come up with these model 'things'. We are supposed to use those models with our campaigns or that Decision Engine 'thing'. But what is a predictive model? How is it built? What insight can you get from it and how will that help you?

A statistical predictive model is a combination of mathematical formulae and rules that are applied on your customer data to determine the likelihood of a particular behaviour or outcome. In other words, a way of predicting what the target recipient of your marketing activity will do in response to that activity based on the data you already know about them. That probably still seems a little confusing so let's break it down a little further.

Data

Let's start with the customer data. You need to get an understanding of what data you have got for your customers as this will determine what you can predict. You will also need to understand its quality. This means is it up-to-date, is it clean or could it have been corrupted in some way? Preparing the data for building the model is probably about 60% of the statisticians' job. For example, if you want to build a response model, which is a model that will select those people most likely to respond to your campaign, you will have to have recorded who responded to you last time to build the model. This is one reason reporting and recording what happened is so important.

For statistical modelling, the data is generally held in 'tables' in your customer database. With the advent of Big Data, this has changed quite a bit, but for now we will describe how most of the 'older' modelling tools do it.

A table is made up of a number of 'rows' which have a number of 'columns'. Each row generally represents one customer record. The customer data is usually split up amongst several tables to speed up the process of accessing the data. For the purposes of this explanation, however, we will assume that there is only one table and it has all your customer data in it. Each customer has one row or record. The columns will be where each 'attribute' of the customer is stored.

First Name	Last Name	Postcode	Hair Colour	Eye Colour	Height	Hobby
Jo	Bloggs	TG34 6PL	Brown	Brown	6'2"	Stamps
Mike	Brown	PL16 1PX	Blond	Blue	5'2"	Books
George	White	TG34 6PL	Brown	Brown	5'9"	?

COLUMN OR ATTRIBUTE → (Hair Colour)

OUTCOME → (Hobby)

ROW OR RECORD → (data rows)

Predictions

In the example above, we want to determine what hobby someone is likely to have. By comparing the attributes of customers who have the outcome that we want, we can see if there is a pattern that would indicate that likelihood.

> With the data available in this simple example, we can say:
>
> "If Postcode = TG34 6PL and Hair Colour = Brown and Eye Colour = Brown then Hobby 90% likely to be Stamps."

The reason we would not say 100% is that there is another attribute – Height – that does not match. But also, if you have 100% likelihood then the outcome generally already exists and you have only predicted what is already known as the outcome. This is why the statisticians must be very careful when selecting which attributes to use for the model – this sort of model is known as self-fulfilling.

Statisticians get a little help in the model building effort from predictive mining tools. This is software that uses computing power to calculate the formulae of the models. The predictive mining tools do this sort of comparison across millions of rows of data with hundreds of attributes. The example has also just done a simple comparison; what the tools will do is apply other mathematical formulae to single and combinations of attributes in order to find the optimum prediction. When you are presented with the results from a mining project you may see that there are different names for the different model types. These are just different methodologies to the mathematics that you may hear mentioned. Examples include: neural nets, decision trees, logistic regression and genetic algorithms.

The outcome is the attribute you are looking for in a certain condition as a marketer. For example, this may be the likelihood to respond to your communication, purchase a product or take up a service. If purchasing a product, you can also predict how much they are likely to spend if it is a variable price. *However, you can only make predictions based on past data*. If you want to predict something new, you have to find a proxy to model against or just use some rules to select your customers. Our advice, if you are new to this, is to seek guidance from your statistician as to the best course of action. They will know your data best. There is no fixed wrong or right approach; it will vary a lot with each situation. If you are really stuck, then we suggest some test campaigns to find out what might work.

In our ICE world, we want to understand the audience's ordinary world and their attitudes to certain things in order to know what we need to do to engage them. For our banking example that we refer to throughout section 4, we might want to understand the audience's behaviour with regard to taking risk. This will tell us what level of insurance they might want with their new home or if they would be interested in our savings products aligned with the mortgage that they may want.

Before you use the model, it is a good idea to see what insight building the model has produced. During the processes of preparing the data for the modelling process the mining tools will analyse the data, which produces insight that you can use. Be aware that not all attributes are created equal; some will have a higher predictive power than others. One of the outputs of producing the model should be a ranking of the top ten most predictive attributes. This is important to you as a marketer as it may provide useful information for your communication. For example, it may be that the timing of the communication is the strongest predictor to a response; i.e. Wednesday afternoon is the best time to contact people. When briefing for a model build, therefore, it is important to ask for the model analysis as this may change what, how and when you communicate.

Now that you understand what data you have at your disposal and which models could be applied, this brings us to how the model is used. Let's say you build a response model – i.e. a model designed to select customers most likely to respond to your campaign. You have 100 potential customers who you wish to target, but it is not optimal to send your communication to everyone. Firstly, it is not an efficient use of your resources, (even if e-mail is virtually free!); secondly, and more importantly for those who are not likely to respond, you are potentially only upsetting them and damaging your brand value. Finally, you want to attract their interest and the communication needs to be welcomed and appreciated. In order to pick the right number and the right customers to send

your communication to, you must look at the 'gains curve' of the model.

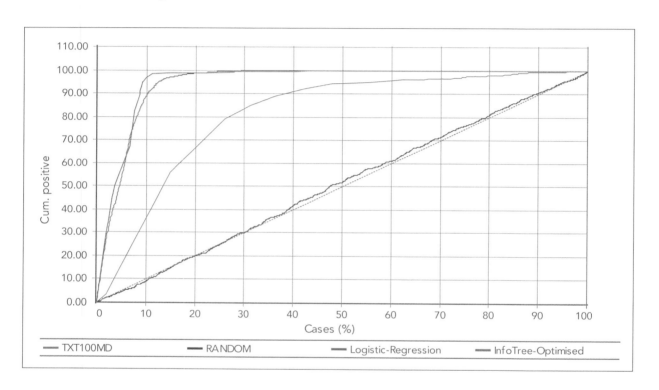

In the diagram above, the straight line that runs diagonally across the chart represents what would happen if you randomly selected customers or the average response. The curved lines represent different modelling methods that produce different 'strength' of model or predictive power. The 'gains curve' is the difference between the random line and the lines produced by the models. So in this example, by selecting 10% of your

customer base you will get to 90% of the people who are likely to respond to you.

This basic example shows you how predictive modelling makes for more intelligent marketing with better outcomes. Hopefully, it will not all seem like some dark art that is occurring in the statisticians' corner now and you will be able to deliver more effective marketing using predictive models.

NOTES

APPENDIX

2

2

Glossary of Terms

Content Marketing – The use of content within any marketing activity, campaign or programme regardless of channel, media or approach.

Content Strategy – The overarching plan for delivering a content marketing programme (for breadth of interpretations see section 2, chapter 1).

Content Decisioning – Using the data that can be generated about a piece of content and the content consumers' content history to decide which piece of content you should serve next.

Audience Engagement Strategy – The integrated approach to engaging the audience (prospects and customers) through all customer touch-points that takes the audience on a structured journey towards a defined goal.

Content Pillars – The themes that are derived from the point of mutuality from which specific items of content can then be produced.

Segments – The traditional approach to defining different target customer groups, typically around factors such as age, sex, income, etc.

Personas – The more mature approach of defining target customer groups that seeks to understand the goals, understanding, attitudes and barriers the audiences may have.

Point of Mutuality – The core subject matter that both your brand and your audience can mutually engage about.

ICE (Intelligent Customer Engagement) – The model for re-aligning your business around engaging your audience using content within an Audience Engagement Strategy.

ESP (Engagement Strategy Planner) – ESP More commonly known as e-mail service provider, but in this book we mean the tool that will allow you to define your engagement strategy maps.

NPS (Net Promoter Score) – 'Net Promoter Score' is a customer loyalty metric developed by (and a registered trademark of) Fred Reichheld, Bain & Company, and Satmetrix. It was introduced by Reichheld in his 2003 *Harvard Business Review* article 'One Number You Need to Grow'. NPS can be as low as −100 (everybody is a detractor) or as high as +100 (everybody is a promoter). An NPS that is positive (i.e. higher than zero) is felt to be good, and an NPS of +50 is excellent. Net Promoter Score (NPS) measures the loyalty that exists between a provider and a consumer.

MRM (Marketing Resource Management) – provides the software infrastructure to support marketing operations management. marketing operations management is the alignment of people, process and technology to support marketing activities and improve marketing effectiveness. MRM generally refers to technology for the areas of planning, design and production within marketing and MRM solutions do not provide the analytics, decisioning and automated execution capabilities for personalised marketing across channels. MRM is a subset of Enterprise Marketing Management (EMM) solutions which provide more complete capabilities for all of the functions and roles within marketing.

CRM (Customer Relationship Management) – Customer Relationship Management (CRM) is a system for managing a company's interactions with current and future customers. It involves using technology to organise, automate and synchronise sales, marketing, customer service, and technical support.

Big Data – A popularised term used to refer to the large volumes of data that is collected through everyday interactions. This can include purchase history, searches, website traffic, and e-mail open rates etc., which all relate back to customers.

Net Present Value – In finance, the net present value (NPV) or net present worth (NPW) of a timed series of cash flows, both incoming and outgoing, is defined as the sum of the present values (PVs) of the individual cash flows of the same entity. NPV can be described as the 'difference amount' between the sums of discounted: cash inflows and cash outflows. It compares the present value of money today to the present value of money in the future, taking inflation and returns into account. The NPV of a sequence of cash flows takes as input the cash flows and a discount rate or discount

curve and outputs a price. In a customer context it is about looking at the present value of a customer, predicting the likely sales, and then discounting those back to the current day's value in order to calculate the NPV of a customer.

Customer (vs. Audience) – Someone who has purchased from your business and that you have an on-going relationship with.

Audience (vs. Customer) – Someone who you need to engage with to meet your goals.

Prospect – Someone who you would like to make a purchase from your business.

Inbound Marketing (vs. Outbound) – Inbound marketing is when a customer or prospect initiates the contact with a brand.

Outbound Marketing (vs. Inbound) – Outbound is when a brand sends a message to a customer or prospect.

Editorial Calendar – The live planning tool defining what content needs to be produced by when.

Laydown Plan – The live planning tool defining when the content will be published and how. This may be through a campaign.

Contact Strategy – The rules of engagement with an audience. For example, you may only contact the customers once every month by phone, and once a week by e-mail.

Next-Best-Action – 'Next-best-action marketing (also known as best next action or next best activity), as a special case of next-best-action decision-making, is a customer-centric marketing paradigm that considers the different actions that can be taken for a specific customer and decides on the 'best' one. The next-best-action (an offer, proposition, service, etc.) is

The Intelligent Marketing Institute

determined by the customer's interests and needs on the one hand, and the marketing organisation's business objectives and policies on the other. The campaigning approach first creates a proposition for a product or service and then attempts to find interested and eligible prospects for that proposition.

Content Curation – The process of obtaining pre-existing content from third party sources around a specific topic and using it for your own purposes, as opposed to creating the content yourself, e.g. sourcing articles from newspapers and using them in your communications.

Audience Engagement Map – The structured journey based on the content pillars.

Acknowledgements

The authors extend their thanks to **Hugh Wilson**, Professor of Strategic Marketing, Cranfield School of Management and **Moira Clark**, Professor of Strategic Marketing at Henley Business School and Director of the Henley Centre for Customer Management. They both provided considerable help in formulating the principles of the maturity model in section 2 and for the research that validated this model. Thanks are also due to **Dr Chris Bailey** for her research into O2 and sales through service best practice case study and **Swati Phadnis** for her statistical work on the model.

The **Intelligent Marketing** Institute

Website: www.timihub.com
E-mail: aly.richards@timihub.com &
                  scott.mclean@timihub.com
Twitter: @CxGenius & @ScottNLMcLean
LinkedIn group: http://linkd.in/1qzP3Rx